THE MONEY SHOT

In *The Money Shot*, author, Crystal Gifford empowers professional athletes with great financial decision-making tools, which are fostered through her wise counsel and perspectives often broader than your own. Dr. Gifford builds a strong foundation of awareness as she offers simple steps to avoid the missteps that frequently derail pro-athletes in being empowered in financial matters. Her contribution to pro-sport financial literacy is a great tool for any player coming into unique or unexpected levels of wealth. Gifford is gifted with the education, experience, vision and dedication for blessing many people. In a confusing world, one truth can be worth thousands of dollars; she shares the truth about true financial prosperity available to young pro-athletes who need the support and guidance necessary to make the best, long-term decisions about how to manage and grow a unique opportunity of amassing great wealth.

—**Loren Fogelman**, Expert Sports Performance
https://expertsportsperformance.com

The Money Shot is just what the sub-title says it is: "The Professional Athlete's Financial Playbook to Make the Big Time Last a Lifetime." It is a uniquely detailed guide for athletes that covers many layers of the life you will lead once you claim that "Pro" status. Dr. Gifford talks "straight talk." She is sometimes sassy, sometimes funny, sometimes challenging, but always honest about difficult topics you will encounter in the process of managing your uniquely acquired extensive wealth. Things like the very "business" of your life, frightening topics such as taxes and insurance and estates. And at the core of it all lies the wisdom and direction to save your money and manage it for your *future self.* Although written for professional athletes, this book would benefit anyone highly focused on a sound financial future

A big question I had was why a book such as Crystal's was necessary in our lives. The answer lies within as she introduces the book with a story of two dissimilar professional football players and how different their lives were after retirement from the game. Chronicles of every nature are rife with the stories of pro-players who find their rock-star lives in turmoil because too much money too soon was not within their ability to effectively manage. There are also myriad stories about other sports stars who made choices that best benefited their future, and allowed them to continue to live the luxury lifestyles they earned.

Gifford is visible, vulnerable and richly honest in a conversation with pro-players that will set her wisdom on fire in their hearts. Within the pages of *The Money Shot*, readers will come face to face with biggest challenge you will experience once claiming the "Pro" status. Finances. She is clear that **now** is the time to learn how to manage your money in a way that prepares you for the eventual transition from your game into the next chapter of life. She boldly awakens readers to the reality that making it to the big leagues takes a lot of discipline and brings financial responsibility as well. Don't put it off one more day! Read this book and discover how to make the most of the unique wealth your career can provide.

—**T. R. Stearns**, EdS, Retired Superintendent of Schools

THE
MONEY
SHOT

*The Professional Athlete's Financial Playbook
to Make the Big Time Last a Lifetime*

DR. CRYSTAL D. GIFFORD, CFP®

New York

THE MONEY SHOT
The Professional Athlete's Financial Playbook to Make the Big Time Last a Lifetime

Published in New York, New York, by Morgan James Publishing. Morgan James and The Entrepreneurial Publisher are trademarks of Morgan James, LLC. www.MorganJamesPublishing.com

The Morgan James Speakers Group can bring authors to your live event. For more information or to book an event visit The Morgan James Speakers Group at www.TheMorganJamesSpeakersGroup.com.

Shelfie

A free eBook edition is available with the purchase of this print book.

CLEARLY PRINT YOUR NAME ABOVE IN UPPER CASE

Instructions to claim your free eBook edition:
1. Download the Shelfie app for Android or iOS
2. Write your name in **UPPER CASE** above
3. Use the Shelfie app to submit a photo
4. Download your eBook to any device

ISBN 978-1-63047-837-7 paperback
ISBN 978-1-63047-839-1 eBook
ISBN 978-1-63047-838-4 hardcover
Library of Congress Control Number:
2015916821

Cover Design by:
Rachel Lopez
www.r2cdesign.com

Interior Design by:
Bonnie Bushman
The Whole Caboodle Graphic Design

In an effort to support local communities and raise awareness and funds, Morgan James Publishing donates a percentage of all book sales for the life of each book to Habitat for Humanity Peninsula and Greater Williamsburg.

Get involved today, visit
www.MorganJamesBuilds.com

Habitat for Humanity®
Peninsula and
Greater Williamsburg
Building Partner

DEDICATION

THIS BOOK IS dedicated to all of my Finance and Economics students at Central State University. You taught me how much my work is needed and set the foundation for me to serve athletes in the way I do today. I grew up with you. I will never forget you.

TABLE OF CONTENTS

FOREWORD

BELIEVE IN THE beauty and power of your dream, but make sure to have a back-up plan—yes, a Plan B! This is a cornerstone of my career, and one which I believe is noted throughout Crystal's message to you in *The Money Sho*t. Before landing my dream job, kicking for the Kansas City Chiefs, I was cut eleven times by eight teams. I never knew for sure I would ever break through as an NFL kicker, so I decided my back up plan was to focus on my education, attending Dartmouth, working as a legislative aide for Senator John Chafee of Rhode Island on environmental issues, and Senator Bob Packwood on Senate Commerce, Science and Transportation Committee—Aviation Safety. My Plan B was working hard and also listening to my gut. Crystal writes in her book about taking the time to do "trial runs" of the other things in life you think you would enjoy: the great lesson is that learning what is NOT right for you is just as important, and you only can find that out by taking risks and committing with all your heart, because the lesson of whether its right or wrong is clear only when you throw all of your best into something.

Crystal also encourages readers to find others whom you can trust to pave the way to make the best financial decisions in your life. Find your mentors. Surround yourself with people that bring out your best, and for whom you do the same. Although he was not my own source for financial decisions, I found a mentor in my next-door neighbor, who just happened to be Supreme Court Justice, Byron "Whizzer" White. Justice White had led the NFL in rushing twice, and had a remarkable perspective on balance in life. He influenced many decisions I made— by his example as much as his words. He was a man of few words, but everything was about focus, passion, and serving a higher purpose. I was disconcerted by being cut so many times, and remember asking his advice. He said, "*You will be respected not by anything you say, but by being a consistent performer on the field. Just shut up, do your job, and you will gain respect.*" Not only did he give wise counsel, but his example alone gave me inspiration to aim higher. Find those people who inspire you, and surround yourself with them… they magnetize you to greatness!

At Dartmouth College, I was a theater and drama major at first, which helped me understand how my mind and emotions worked under the spotlight and pressure, but switched to Government, which led to a great opportunity to work with Senator Chafee, another great role model who was a true Korean War hero, featured in a book by the great Historian, Stephen Ambrose (famous among others for "*Band of Brothers*"), and College Hall of Fame Wrestler at Yale.

I looked at my work with Senator Chafee as what I planned to do if I didn't make it big in the NFL; an 18-year career in the NFL was not even on the horizon at that point! I found being successful in such a uniquely challenging, powerful, stimulating environment as the NFL requires more than planning; it requires unparalleled **Focus**, great **Persistence**, discovering untapped **Passion**, and a complete **Commitment to the Game**. I refused to give up on my dream, and not knowing when or if I would ever make it, I planned to continue my work in the Senate and try out for as many teams as it took, because each experience, whether in the Senate or being cut in the

NFL, helped me learn to grow from fear… to focus, to confidence, to command, to mastery. Along the way, I came to recognize that in my commitment to make my dream come true, I got better and better at managing both my preparation and the game itself. How does this apply to your financial decisions? You have to recognize the financial opportunity that lies before you and be as committed and persistent to the preservation and expansion of your wealth as you do to what is on average a 3 to 4 year career, which even at its best, ends at 40. Just as the game is a unique challenge that builds your emotional and physical muscle, filled with electric opportunities to prove yourself in front of over 70,000 screaming fans a few feet away, thousands often rooting against you with very creative, colorful words designed just for you, *so is the process of building your money muscle.* You learn never to take things for granted, and to never stop working to improve.

In myriad places throughout *The Money Shot*, Dr. Gifford shares a thought I frequently held in my pursuit of making it in the NFL, and achieving a record-setting level of success: "*You have to learn a lot about yourself.*" One of the aspects of her book I enjoyed the most was her posing important questions in the pursuit of self-awareness. If you don't know what makes you burn with desire, you won't have a "why" big enough to keep you on course. Come to know that our God is big enough, and our Purpose is big enough to transcend all our challenges!

Dr. Gifford also speaks of the privilege of developing a sense of community and sharing your wealth. Today, I do enjoy that privilege—and that is the correct word—realizing that Life makes the most sense in the relentlessly beautiful, empathetic music of giving back to our community, connecting with and helping others. I have been frequently quoted for the following belief: **"It's not the Brightness of the Spotlight on you, but the Intensity of the Light within you that is the true measure of a human being."** A man is not measured by what he has, but by what he gives away. A leader is only a leader

xiv | THE MONEY SHOT

not by taking power from others, but by inspiring power in them. One is a bully; *the other is a Champion*. The notion of service and the idea of solving problems that need to be solved bring music to life. For me, it's inspiring kids to realize when they are sitting at that desk in the classroom, that they are working toward discovering and finding their own Purpose unique to their God-given gifts, and that they deserve to have a life that is an extension of their own powerful God-given abilities. When kids feel that purpose, they feel powerful and important in the best way, not in an ego-based way, but an infinite Spiritual way that can never be taken away. The greatest gift is using your success to share that message to kids, which pro football players and all high profile athletes and entertainers can do. An encouraging few seconds with a young person—or even adult—can help change a life sometimes. Just last week in Kansas City, someone came up to me in the Westin Crown Center Hotel and said that one day 30 years ago, when I spoke to a group of inner city kids with my teammate Kevin Ross, one young man whose mother was in prison, and had no father determined to spend his life inspiring and helping others… and that man was standing right in front of me. Today, he buys homes to help people transition from prison to a life of higher Purpose. Can you imagine any better reward than hearing that? And your own stories like that are waiting for you as well! Just have your Plan B so you are ready for anything!

Listen to Crystal! Take up the gauntlet and find the fire burning inside to utilize your unique opportunity to amass and organize the kind of wealth that allows you the choice and ***privilege*** to live a lifestyle that not only pleases you, but provides beautiful and practical encouragement for others. I fervently believe a true champion shares his power with others—in name and deed. You can be a Steward of the Game, but you also have the rare opportunity to manage the resources made available to you in such a manner that you can step into a place of Leadership and Gratitude by living as large *in heart* in Life as you do in the Game—a Steward of the game of Life, sharing a sense of purpose and power.

> *Find congruency between your life and*
> *the way you play your chosen sport.*

I agree wholeheartedly with Crystal's message: feel good about living a lifestyle you deserve for the work and excellence you put into your sport, but at the end of the day, managing your wealth in a manner that allows you to give to everyone that matters in life. The financial decisions I made relative to my sports earnings now allow me to encourage others and make the world a better place, and that is what life is all about for me! I have a great sense of pride and fulfillment in working with the Homeless, with Homeless Vets, with Native youth, in Champions against Bullying, and in #StrongerSafer Sports, creating a future where head injuries do not permanently risk an athlete's brain health. I could have done none of this had I not followed four of the key elements which Crystal so astutely delivers in *The Money Shot*:

1. ***Believe in your dream*** and respect the privilege to play sport a the highest level.
2. ***Know yourself*** – discover what you want in life as you take the next step after a sports career
3. ***Surround yourself with people who bring out your best,*** be they mentors of quality friends who you in turn bring the best out in. Live an amazing and balanced lifestyle.
4. ***Create enough to share in some future philanthropic community adventure*** that plays a consistent music of ***Gratitude***.

Nick Lowery transcends any category.

Hall of Famer, Ivy League scholar, presidential aide, author and poet, teacher, and philanthropist, the Kansas City Chiefs Hall of Famer was the most accurate kicker in NFL History.

Nick's story is about persistence that leads to Focus, Passion, and Purpose. He won the NFL Man of the Year award for both the Kansas City Chiefs and New York Jets.

The Harvard and Dartmouth graduate is the winner of the NFL Player's humanitarian award, the Byron Whizzer White award.

For information about Nick's speaking or community work, contact Nick at Nick@Loweryspeaks.com or visit...

www.nicklowery.org

ACKNOWLEDGEMENTS

IN THE CREATION of a book, there is never one person who should get credit. While I get credit as the author, this project did not happen alone. Without some key players I may have never gotten this project out of my laptop and into the hands of those who need it. Thank you to all of you who contributed, those mentioned here, and those who added value in intangible ways.

Topher Morrison and my fellow Key Person of Influence business accelerator cohorts, you made me stop in my tracks when I was writing about another topic I love but that did not serve my market. Thank you for pushing me and making me see that my athletes needed what I have to offer in a way that could meet them in their private spaces, and for boosting my confidence that this market cares what I have to say. This may not be a two crap book but its contents can be digested for mental nourishment, so I think that counts.

Anna Weber, how could I have made this a go without your support? Thank you so much for keeping me on track. Because of your help, this manuscript got into print instead of staying with me and serving no one. Your guidance every step of the way has been invaluable, and I am forever grateful that you showed up in my life as my editor and now my friend.

To the many athletes I spoke with and asked you if sections of the book made sense, thank you for your honest feedback. It was extremely helpful for a girl like me who knows finance well, but stopped at high school basketball when it comes to the intricacies of the athlete life. Your input is what makes this book something athletes can relate to and live by when it comes to their financial journey. Thank you so much.

Thank you, Duke Preston, for answering all my questions about the needs you see not being met for athletes. I know you were busy but you always answered my emails and texts and your input has proven to be super-insightful in the process of completing this project.

To my wonderful son, Andrew, you were awesome when I was hunkered down writing and kept calling you in to ask you sports related questions. Your patience helped turn my thoughts into content useful for my athletes. Without you, I would have spent so much more time asking Google how everything worked and never be sure if it was accurate. Not only did you make my job easier, you helped my confidence in its value as well. Thanks for your support and help… and all of the meals you brought to me while I worked away and would have otherwise forgotten to eat.

To my publisher team for coordinating and organizing all that I need to do to get this book into the hands of those who need it, thank you for keeping this scattered girl on target—with a plan. I am so happy we decided to work together.

To my dad, who continues to be my #1 supporter in everything I do, I know if I ever want someone to buy in to what I am working on, all I have to do is tell you about it. Your famous words How can I get in on that will ring in my ears all the days of my life. No matter what path I take, you have always been there ready to jump in with both feet and do whatever you can to help. I love you, Dad.

And to my new friends I have met along the way as we prepared to complete this manuscript, thank you for making this a joyful journey. I am excited for our future together.

PREFACE

JOEL BOARDED THE plane with anticipation, excitement. Even though in size he was typical of a large, muscular football player, Joel had a case of butterflies in his stomach so strong you would think it was mating season. He pinched himself more than once. *Is it really possible that this dream I have worked for almost all my life is really coming true?*

As he began to put away his new duffle bag that sported his team name into the overhead bins in first class, Round four kept swirling in Joel's head. *I really made round four! First class. Wow! Is this what a $2.5 million contract looks like?* His signing bonus alone was more than his parents had ever made during his life. The young man had never flown first class before and he wondered if the airlines would charge him for the blanket and pillow that lay in his seat. It was just over a four-hour flight ahead of him. *Is this real?* Joel thought as he pinched himself one more time to be sure. His agent assured Joel he would pick him up at the airport in San Francisco.

"Breath, Joel!" he reminded himself. With a final glance around to be sure no one heard him talking to himself or tell him he couldn't sit there, Joel settled into seat 2A. He was just getting settled in when another man, equally as large, and clearly just as young, came onto the plane carrying a bag full of food and drinks, magazines, and what looked like a bottle of rum. Joel watched as he took a few minutes to get settled with all the stuff he was carrying. Finally, as he put the last piece away, Joel noticed the other duffle bag had the same logo as the one Joel had received from his agent just three days prior.

"You're playing with the 49ers, man?" Joel asked.

"Yeah man. I almost missed this flight, too. That signing bonus was tight so we turnt up last night to celebrate my last night in the 202, and we did it big!"

"Good deal, bro," Joel replied. "It looks like we will be seeing a lot of each other." Joel pulled out his draft card to confirm his team camaraderie. "Cornerback. What's your spot?"

"Man, I was a quarterback all my life, but I am running with the backs now. I guess it's cool, though. I'll get that starting spot soon enough."

"Word," replied Joel.

"I'm Brandon, by the way." A loud thud echoed through first class from the contact of their hands as they greeted as if they were boys back in the hood.

"Joel. Good to meet you, man. Can you believe this is all happening?"

Joel and Brandon continued their conversation over the next four hours, sleeping some, reading magazines, listening to music, and talking when the moment hit. They agreed to have each other's backs as they transitioned to their new journey, and were both very happy to know at least they had one friend on the team already.

When they arrived in San Francisco, it was a whirlwind of agents, photos, fans, and media interviews. Both young men were swept up in the introductions, attention, and getting acquainted with their new lifestyle.

The next day on the field, Joel noticed Brandon looked a little tired, but his performance seemed ok so he didn't bother to ask how he was doing. Joel needed to focus on his own game today, and he planned to kill it, and play like he'd been in the pros for years. Some of his teammates commented he had a determination in his eyes they hadn't seen in many rookies.

In the locker room, Joel met more of his teammates and had a chance to interact. One of them, a little older than the others, introduced himself with some southern charm. Joel wasn't familiar with this depth of warmness. He liked the guy; Chris was his name. Chris welcomed Joel and told him to beware.

"This all looks nice in the beginning, but fail to take care of yourself and you will have a short-lived limelight." Chris warned. "So many young fellas come through here all excited. They've never made money like this before, and because of that burning thrill, they blow it all faster than it can even hit their bank accounts. People start reaching their hands out and we feel the pressure to be liked and start putting your money in hands that have no mind taking from us."

At first Joel wanted to run. He heard this same message from his parents, and his professors. Even his agent tried to lecture him a little about money. *Now, my teammates are lecturing me too?* Something about Chris made him keep listening this time.

"You can enjoy your money, son. You've earned it. But don't forget you have a whole life to live and this is just a short part of it. Here's the number to the financial strategist I hired. I gave her office a call and she set me up. If I left the game today, I'd never want for anything again. I can go out there every day and play like I mean it; play because I love it. That's the secret to why I've lasted so long."

Joel took the card from Chris and put it in his bag. At that moment, he had no intention to call the number… but just in case. Besides, his momma raised him right and he wasn't going to be rude and throw away the card in front of Chris. Joel thanked him and went about the business of getting dressed for the team introductions dinner.

As the year progressed, both Joel and Brandon excelled in their positions. Brandon even went on to be the team MVP for the Special Teams. It was looking good that they would both make the team and be on pace to start by the second year. They were happy, and so were the coaches.

During the year, Joel had followed Chris's advice and called up the financial strategist. By now, he had a clear plan and it was implemented so all he had to do was keep performing and his money was going to work for him. He had tried to drag Brandon with him, but Brandon wanted nothing to do with someone who was going to "Tell me how I can spend my money!" Joel even met Brandon once when out for dinner with his financial strategist, but Brandon didn't want to talk about money at all, so they talked sports and girls, and stats.

The advisor gave Brandon her card at the end of the night and urged him, "If you ever change your mind, give me a call. If I am not the right person to work with you, I can connect you with someone who is. Don't let your talent go to waste. You only make this type of money for a short period of time; if you don't manage it properly, it won't last long."

The two young men went on to enjoy their careers as starters, and while neither of them had six-figure endorsements like Nike knocking on their doors, they did manage to land a few good, deals. The extra money was great, and Joel often rewarded himself with something new when he landed extra, unexpected money.

"I see you are not using that advisor, Brandon said one day in the locker room."

"I am, actually. Why do you say that?" Joel asked.

"Ain't no finance person going to let you buy yourself a souped up Escalade," Brandon scoffed with a grunt.

"Actually, I buy what I want." Joel replied. "I just do it within some clear boundaries she helped me establish so I am straight on everything I buy. I know exactly what impact each purchase has on my future. And when I want to have some fun, I do. If I want to make it rain, I can, but I don't. I just have a system that lets me decide what I want more in each moment, and I call her when I am not sure."

"You're crazy, man." Brandon laughed. "But good luck with the financial prison thing she's got you locked in."

Joel didn't argue. He had seen Brandon partying and buying shots for the whole bar. Oh, he was popular, that was for sure, but Joel had not needed to visit the bank and ask for money even once, and he knew Brandon had a regular line with the bank that allowed him to buy what he wanted—even long before he even signed his next contract.

It is shocking, Joel thought as he boarded the plane to go visit his family, *how much of that signed contract I never actually got to see. Who knew taxes, living expenses, and fees could be so high!* Growing up in a poor family, Joel had always thought if he ever made over a million dollars he would never have to think about money again. Now, he mostly didn't have to worry about money anymore, but he found he needed to be aware. It was too easy to get caught up in the fun and pleasure, and having everyone like you in the bar did feel cool while it was happening. He had done that a couple times—rounds for the bar—but he kept imagining the faces of his future sons looking at him, wanting a new bike or to join a traveling sports team and decided if he was going to make it rain it was going to be on the people he loved!

During a bi-week, Joel showed up at his mom's house for a surprise visit, with tons of gifts in hand. He had so much he had to ship most of it to a friend's house and pick it up on the way. Nieces, nephews, mom, dad, brothers, sisters… he had such a large family, and had gotten something for everyone. His favorite part was the check he was able to hand his mom when they settled down from all the excitement that evening.

"Joel, I can't take this, baby. You worked hard for this." His mom shook her head.

But Joel quietly explained to her how he had been working with a financial strategist, and how she showed him exactly how the plan affected his future ability to help his mom, and could do so with no worries about his own future.

"Moms," Joel started in, "Let me worry about that! In fact, my financial strategist wants to meet you so you can know I am being taken care of. She said she may have some ways to help you and Pops, too. She's got a whole team of people who can help players like me understand money, and help their families learn about it too. You will like her."

With tears in her eyes, Joel's mom knew he was going to be ok. For the first time Joel could remember, his mom had a glimmer in her that made him think she may just be dreaming a little bit of doing something nice for herself and his dad. His parents had never been on a real vacation before so Joel was able to experience great joy in this special moment of knowing his mom, who never asked for anything and always just gave to others, was finally going to get to enjoy something for herself. It was a great visit.

Meanwhile, Brandon headed home, too. He arrived on Thursday, but met up with some friends first and had a few drinks. He finally pulled in to his mom's house around 2:00 AM and since everyone was asleep, his nephew let him in and he crashed in his old room until the next morning.

Brandon was happy to see his mom, but he felt uncomfortable here now. The luxuries he had been enjoying sure weren't found in the home he grew up in. It was a nice home, but it was clear it needed a little work. Brandon's mom had worked two jobs all his life, and she kept up the house, but she was never really able to add any improvements to it.

As he wandered around the house the next morning noticing all the little things that needed fixed, Brandon realized he could easily fix these things for his mom if he just gave up one party night a month. He vowed in that moment that he was going to send his mom some money with his next contract pay. He was out for now, and the bank was fronting his trip home, but for sure he was going to take care of his mom the next chance he had.

They had a nice visit, and Brandon's family was so happy to see him. They took pictures, and he got to make his nieces and nephews look like super stars to their friends. Everyone had a good time and Brandon was leaving a few days later, he told his mom not to worry, I'm going to take care of you so you don't have to work so much just to run the house. She smiled and thanked him, but said, "Don't worry about your ole mom, I am making my way just fine."

As their NFL careers progressed, both Brandon and Joel continued to be successful; Brandon lasted six years in his position before it was time for him to start thinking about life after football. Joel's career was slightly longer, with seven years participation with the team. Both men were eligible for their pension. They could start collecting the first part at the age of 35, and the second at age 45. That is, of course, if they contributed to it during their playing years. Joel had; Brandon had not.

When it was time to begin looking at what was next in life, Joel took a drive in his new convertible to his financial strategist's office. He had traded in the Escalade for something that allowed him to enjoy the open air. He knew he would likely have one or two years left and wanted to get his financial house ready for what was following. Joel left her office pleased that day to know that he was right on target for what he wanted, and well ahead of his original plans which were conservative. He was getting married next fall, so he also wanted to be sure to understand how this all fit in with his lovely bride and the three kids they both wanted. *And wow, that ring... I was the superstar of all her friends with the rock I put on her finger!*

Joel rolled into his new fiancés house after the appointment—proud to know he had taken care of everything. She greeted him with a smile, thinking, *I am the luckiest girl in the world, not because his bank account is lush, but because his heart is rich and he makes me feel like a real woman!*

Brandon also went to see an advisor, finally, when it was time to leave the game. After much prodding, Brandon realized he had no clue what he was going to do next. He knew he was in his final playing year and he figured he better go find out how he was going to continue his party lifestyle. He didn't leave the advisor's office as happy as Joel. Instead of kudos and celebration, Brandon got a huge dose of reality check. After five years in the league, he had spent all his money on parties, exotic cars, bling and expensive items. And the worst part, the one time he tried to invest some money for the future it turned out to be a bad deal and Brandon lost everything he had invested and even owed money to get out of the deal. Right then he had decided investing doesn't work and he was going to live it up.

He had some assets, and the advisor assured him at least he had a way to make his mess a little less messy by selling some of the fancy cars he owned. But Brandon had not set himself up with any assets that would generate income, and his final pay would be the last chance he had at preparing himself for a future.

Luckily, several of the cars still had value, and by liquidating them, Brandon was able to repay almost all of the debt he owed. He wasn't happy about this, but he had finally grown up a bit and realized that the way he was living could not last forever. His big house he could keep, right? He was really hoping to keep that. The problem was, in order to keep the house he had to have income sufficient to pay the outrageous taxes every year. Taxes in California are no joke, he realized, so in the end, Brandon decided to liquidate all of his assets except his favorite one car, which he would keep to trade in for something more reasonable.

Joel went on after his career to develop a foundation helping young men without fathers learn how to play sports. He was proud of the life he had created. His wife and three children lived a very nice lifestyle. They were in a suburban town because it had the best private schools and they could be home with their kids every day when they got out of school, go eat school lunches with them, and take fascinating vacations that many others their age could not afford. It was a comfortable life, and the free time they enjoyed to do what they wanted was the most rewarding. Because of this extra time, both Joel and his wife became well known in the community for making a big difference. Instead of working, they used their time to build business ventures and also to give back to their community. Joel still sees his financial strategist at least once a year, and each year he gives her the biggest hug and thanks her for keeping finances **real** with him so he could live the life he wanted. Life for Joel remains good.

Brandon also found a way to make his life good. He didn't have the flashy cars anymore, and his home was a modest 2500 square foot home just outside the city. He liked it there. He had also found a wife and was very happy. They were working on baby number two, and they decided they would stop there. It is expensive to have kids! Brandon found a really good job in the local factory, and because of his hard work and drive, he was already a senior manager. He wasn't overly excited about a 9-5 lifestyle, but it paid the bills and allowed them to have the nice things they had. He was just thankful that he had not gone completely broke and came to his senses in time to save himself some dignity and get his life back in order financially. He knew several ballers who had gone completely bankrupt before they admitted getting professional help with money was a good idea.

He had learned his lesson well, and Brandon volunteered one day per week after work to meet with a group of young athletes who were aspiring to go pro. He used his influence as a Pro in the NFL to get their attention, and he shared his stories with them, teaching basic money principles so when they grow up they could live a life that is financially sound, whether they worked a job like him or going pro and having a chance to really set themselves up for whatever they wanted.

Joel and Brandon get together every couple of years between Thanksgiving and New Year's to celebrate the journey they began several years before. They are both happy, and they have a great time reminiscing about the glory days. At the end of the evening, they say their goodbyes and plan for the next one, and Joel picks up the tab.

SECTION I
UNDERSTANDING MONEY

INTRODUCTION

AS YOU READ this, you may have just signed your first contract, you've been in the league for a long time, or maybe you are aspiring to make it to the *Big Time*. While your story may be a little different from Brandon's or Joel's, your contract may be bigger or smaller, your sport may be something else, or you may be in a different stage of the game… the principles learned by Brandon and Joel on their journey are shared in this Playbook for you to learn and grow from their mistakes. Regardless of your current situation, there is time to make changes to improve your financial life.

Throughout this Playbook, we will guide you through the basic concepts you must know in order to create financial freedom, five mistakes you must avoid, and nine strategies to paint a financial picture you can be excited to write home about. Do you want a life like Joel where you are in charge of your days after the game, or will you choose to live like Brandon—party it up during your pro-career and retire to a 9-5 employee lifestyle? The choice is yours. If it is freedom you desire, the answers lie in the pages that follow.

Chapter 1

PAINT YOUR PICTURE OF WEALTH

LET'S TALK A little bit about the relationship you have with money. You've made it to the *Big Time*, so clearly you're okay with making a lot of money, but there's a big difference between making money and having money. Let's face it, when you make a lot of money, it feels good, you feel the flow coming in; you know there's plenty to spend and do what you want. But how many people have won a lottery, hit it big, made big impacts in their lives and then find themselves, yet again, broke within a short period of time once they've hit that big amount?

The problem most people face when dealing with money is that they've never had money or a need to manage it, and then they have an abundance of money suddenly; there's a rush of energy—this hormonal, chemical rush that happens in us, which immediately needs to restore order. In fact, did you know that there is a natural balance of order, or level of happiness, that most people return to after a huge shift in their reality?[1]

This natural tendency means that big changes, whether good or bad, have only a temporary impact on your level of happiness. Unfortunately for many, the desire to get back to that level of joy experienced during a big win sends them on a constant spending cycle, trying to recreate the initial boost felt with the big win. Going pro creates a big win moment, and the signing bonus many receive can feel like it solves every problem in the world we could have... but then reality returns.

Knowing this rush occurs, many times we will have a need to immediately go out and get all the things that we've always wanted. Understand, there are several pieces to this puzzle. First, we want to go out and spend all this newly found money, get all the things that we always wanted but couldn't have before—but now we can. Then we take that idea of spending and buying all the things we want and all of a sudden it expands, like we've never been expanded in this way before. Because we've never been expanded or capable of buying these things before, all of a sudden the feeling gets bigger and bigger; other people are telling us what we should do with the money. Before we know it, we have all these things we think we want, but the truth is, if we really took a moment to decide what we want, many of the things that we've bought wouldn't even be on the list.

The next thing that's likely to happen is we start to notice the way people treat us because of what we now have; it feels good. People respect us more, they pay attention when we have something to say, and a lot of other things start to shift. We start to feel important, significant and needed in the world. These feelings perpetuate the spending and before we know it, we find the more we spend, the more respect we get. Eventually, however, our spending tends to exceed our actual income.

---

1   Coates and Bulman, 1978, http://www.ncbi.nlm.nih.gov/pubmed/690806

It is not because we're an athlete that this happens—the phenomenon is so common it's happened to lottery winners, entertainers, and many others who have inherited millions. People in Hollywood often have this problem. In this Playbook, the focus remains on you as an athlete because you have some special characteristics. You also have the powerful work ethic that many of the people who face sudden wealth don't have.

SO HERE YOU are—working hard, the paychecks start coming in and it's easier and easier to gain access to things, like credit for instance. Now banks line up to loan you money you haven't yet made... because they know you're going to be making it. So you buy and then you expand that purchasing muscle and you move forward. But what's really going on when this happens?

The truth is, what's going on is a psychological shift occurring. You have what you are open and willing to have. So while you've made it to the *Big Time* and are able to earn and create the money and have it flowing to you, you haven't yet gone into the deeper element of questions I often ask many of my clients—to which they are quite surprised to discover the answers. So I want you to ask yourself these questions as you read or listen to *The Money Shot*. Take some time; get out a pen and paper, and write the answers as they come. Maybe you want to take a few deep breaths before you begin to answer them; close your eyes and allow your thoughts to come to you visually, or just open your ears and allow your thoughts to tell you the answers to these questions. How they come is not relevant; however these answers occur to you... just trust the process and record them. You can write them down or you can record them with your voice. How you record your responses is completely up to you. You might find you even get some really cool Twitter posts out of them.

we actually take the time to plot out exactly what that lifestyle looks like; I encourage you to do that here.

- Where do you want to live?
- How many homes do you want to have?
- How many cars?
- How many significant people are going to be involved in your life?
- Is there a significant other?
- Do you want children?
- Is there a family, a mom, a dad, or siblings that you feel obligated to or want to take care of in this lifestyle? Maybe someone who raised you, a guardian? (Note: See our chapter on family to learn how to more effectively help the people you love).

Make sure you write down all your responses, and allow yourself to look at the following as well:

- What kind of vacations do you want to take?
- Where do you want to spend your time?
- What activities do you want to enjoy?
- What does your average life look like, your day, your week, and your month?

Think really deeply about these things; allow those thoughts to help you map out exactly how much income you're going to need to make this lifestyle happen. You might even look at what hobbies you want to have. Some hobbies are more expensive than others. If you have a boat or desire to be on the water, consider the extra expense of water sports and include those figures. If your hobby is playing with toy cars or building out old cars, those are both potentially expensive hobbies.

Look at a hobby such as tennis, maybe it's not as expensive, what about golf? The key point is to remain aware of the hobbies that you have or you want to have after you retire from your sport.

These exercises may seem silly at first glance but trust me, I've worked with them enough that I know the process can make a huge shift and a big difference in the way you keep your money as you accumulate it.

You've worked hard; you deserve it.
Now let's just get clear on the path to keeping it.

You may have heard a thing or two about compound interest in your time, but if you have not started saving, you really haven't heard enough about compound interest! It is one thing to have the information, but hearing its value to the point that you *implement* is where all the gold is. Have you ever heard the phrase "Three feet from the gold?" If you haven't, let me share with you the short version of a story told in more detail in *Think and Grow Rich* by Napoleon Hill.

A gold miner spent all he had and borrowed from friends and family to search for gold. He bought equipment and all the other supplies and materials he needed and started digging. After an exhausting search that led to almost nothing, the miner finally gave up and sold the equipment—for pennies. The buyer, however, knew a little about fault lines and sought out a professional to survey the land. Upon further review, it was determined that the gold the miner had found when he started most likely followed a line that would show up about three feet from where the previous owner had stopped digging. The new buyer, after seeking proper counsel and following through on the advice, discovered his riches… just three feet from where the first miner had stopped.

Knowing about compound interest and not following through to put your money to work for you is like stopping three feet from the gold!!

In case you aren't familiar with compound interest, or have forgotten what you may have been aware of at one time, the next chapter offers a review of this concept. This is especially valuable for you as a pro-athlete; as time is on your side to a greater degree than most others. Review the simple examples in the next chapter, and then assess the distinct advantage you have with the *Big Time* income that comes early in your life.

Chapter 2

WHAT IS COMPOUND INTEREST?

COMPOUND INTEREST IS simply what happens when the money you have saved earns interest, and then the interest earned from saving that money also earns interest!

In the famous book, *The Richest Man in Babylon,* which just happens to one of my personal favorites, George Samuel Clason refers to the original savings as gold coins and then the interest as its babies. So in the beginning you put away some of your gold coins and they go to work for you. Eventually, they start having babies, little soldiers, who also get to work. In the beginning, it takes more gold coins saved to build up all the babies, but at some point, known as the tipping point, there are more babies than the gold coins you originally put away. At this point your money is working for you faster and stronger than any of the gold you could have put away on your own.

I love Clason's simplistic examples and highly recommend you add this book to your reading or audio library. One of my favorite lines from the book is "A portion of all I earn is mine to keep." This doesn't mean to buy things; it means to keep… as in put those golden soldiers and their offspring to work for you. In the book, Clason encourages saving at least 10%. But the focus I want you to have for this saving concept to see what portion of your income you need in order to live your desired lifestyle now, and save the rest.

Because of your special situation, it is quite possible you could mark as much as one-half of what you earn as yours to keep and create a lifestyle for yourself now—and in the future—that most can only dream of. You will learn specifically how to do this in the investing discussion in a later chapter. But for now, back to compound interest, to take a look at what this may look like. Taking the classic example, you consider the concept of a penny that doubles every day:

Would you rather have $1,000,000 or a penny that doubles every day for 30 days?

◇◇◇◇◇◇◇◇◇◇◇◇◇◇

You may at first glance say, "Duh! The $1,000,000 please." But, if you've ever seen this example and understand compound interest, you will know that a penny, doubled every day turns into over $5,000,000. You can Google this and you will find tons of examples where the concept is used to show the power of compound interest. But since you know your money will not double every single day and this may not translate to your earnings, let's look at a couple of wealth building examples specific to you.

First, I ask you to explore what this concept could look like for the average household, and then take a look at how you can use your distinct advantage to make your wealth-building model even better.

Consider yourself first as an average family, with an average of around $80,000 dual income household earnings. If you saved just 10% of your money, you would set aside $8,000 per year. Ideally, you would continue to increase this as your income increased. However, for the purposes of simplicity, you are going to keep this at $8,000 over the life of your working years.

Let's review just how this works, first from the perspective of saving for 30 years but only putting away the money for the first 20. Then we compare, instead, putting it away for the last 20 years, rather than the first 20. Also, you will see how the interest rate affects the total balance. The first example is at 10% interest and the second at 4% interest.

Saving for the first 20 of 30 years at 10%

	Deposit	Interest Earned 10%	Account Balance
Year 1	$8,000	800	$8,800
Year 2	$8,000	1,680	$18,480
Year 3	$8,000	2,648	$29,128
Year 4	$8,000	3,713	$40,841
Year 5	$8,000	4,884	$53,725
Year 6	$8,000	6,172	$67,897
Year 7	$8,000	7,590	$83,487
Year 8	$8,000	9,149	$100,636
Year 9	$8,000	10,864	$119,499
Year 10	$8,000	12,750	$140,249
Year 11	$8,000	14,825	$163,074
Year 12	$8,000	17,107	$188,182
Year 13	$8,000	19,618	$215,800
Year 14	$8,000	22,380	$246,180
Year 15	$8,000	25,418	$279,598
Year 16	$8,000	28,760	$316,358

	Deposit	Interest Earned 10%	Account Balance
Year 17	$8,000	32,436	$356,793
Year 18	$8,000	36,479	$401,273
Year 19	$8,000	40,927	$450,200
Year 20	$8,000	45,820	$504,020
Year 21		50,402	$554,422
Year 22		55,442	$609,864
Year 23		60,986	$670,851
Year 24		67,085	$737,936
Year 25		73,794	$811,729
Year 26		81,173	$892,902
Year 27		89,290	$982,192
Year 28		98,219	$1,080,412
Year 29		108,041	$1,188,453
Year 30		118,845	$1,307,298
Total Saved	$160,000		

Now look at how that changes if you wait 10 years to start saving and save only the last 20 years.

	Deposit	Interest Earned 10%	Account Balance
Year 1	$0	0	$0
Year 2	$0	0	$0
Year 3	$0	0	$0
Year 4	$0	0	$0
Year 5	$0	0	$0
Year 6	$0	0	$0
Year 7	$0	0	$0
Year 8	$0	0	$0
Year 9	$0	0	$0

Year 10	$0	0	$0
Year 11	$8,000	800	$8,800
Year 12	$8,000	1,680	$18,480
Year 13	$8,000	2,648	$29,128
Year 14	$8,000	3,713	$40,841
Year 15	$8,000	4,884	$53,725
Year 16	$8,000	6,172	$67,897
Year 17	$8,000	7,590	$83,487
Year 18	$8,000	9,149	$100,636
Year 19	$8,000	10,864	$119,499
Year 20	$8,000	12,750	$140,249
Year 21	$8,000	14,825	$163,074
Year 22	$8,000	17,107	$188,182
Year 23	$8,000	19,618	$215,800
Year 24	$8,000	22,380	$246,180
Year 25	$8,000	25,418	$279,598
Year 26	$8,000	28,760	$316,358
Year 27	$8,000	32,436	$356,793
Year 28	$8,000	36,479	$401,273
Year 29	$8,000	40,927	$450,200
Year 30	$8,000	45,820	$504,020
Total Saved	$160,000		

You may notice that the same $160,000 was saved by in both examples, but saving in the early stages results in over $800,000 more at the end of the 30-year period. Now, let's change the interest to 14% and see the results: a whopping $3,077,540 for money saved in the first part of the 30-year period, compared to only $830,147 for savings made in the latter part of the same 30 years.

Take note also that a lower interest rate of 4% would change these results dramatically, resulting in only $366,736 for the early saving process and $247,754 for savings made in the latter period. You will discover how to invest at the best interest rates in the investing section.

Another thing to note in the examples above, starting in year 8, at 10%, the interest earned on the funds invested so far exceeds the annual amount saved. That is your tipping point where the babies of your gold coins are doing more than the gold coins you are adding. Delicious!

Let's take a moment now to see how this could work for your particular circumstances, given you could be earning most of your lifetime earnings in the first 3-10 years of your life. You saw the difference it made to put away money early. Let these questions sink in for a few minutes:

- What if you could put away more?
- What if you could take advantage of the fact that you have hit it big long before you even approach the ripe old age of 30, and you have what seems like an eternity before you are at true retirement age.
- Do you have to wait until 65 or older to retire and enjoy life?
- What will you do when you have played out all your days in the game and are ready to move on to something else?

Let's look at an example of what is possible for you, in your life after the game…

Say you make a decision, based on a thorough look at your lifestyle goals, that you could put away $250,000 every year for creating a future for yourself. But, you can only do this for the next five years.

The following charts reflect the impact the more aggressive savings process would have… at 10% interest.

	Deposit	Interest Earned 10%	Account Balance
Year 1	$250,000	25,000	$275,000
Year 2	$250,000	52,500	$577,500
Year 3	$250,000	82,750	$910,250
Year 4	$250,000	116,025	$1,276,275
Year 5	$250,000	152,628	$1,678,903
Year 6	$0	167,890	$1,846,793
Year 7	$0	184,679	$2,031,472
Year 8	$0	203,147	$2,234,619
Year 9	$0	223,462	$2,458,081
Year 10	$0	245,808	$2,703,889
*Year 11	$0	270,389	$2,974,278
Year 12	$0	297,428	$3,271,706
Year 13	$0	327,171	$3,598,877
Year 14	$0	359,888	$3,958,764
Year 15	$0	395,876	$4,354,641
Year 16	$0	435,464	$4,790,105
Year 17	$0	479,010	$5,269,115
Year 18	$0	526,912	$5,796,027
Year 19	$0	579,603	$6,375,629
Year 20	$0	637,563	$7,013,192
Year 21	$0	701,319	$7,714,512
Year 22	$0	771,451	$8,485,963
Year 23	$0	848,596	$9,334,559
Year 24	$0	933,456	$10,268,015
Year 25	$0	1,026,801	$11,294,816
Year 26	$0	1,129,482	$12,424,298
Year 27	$0	1,242,430	$13,666,728
Year 28	$0	1,366,673	$15,033,401
Year 29	$0	1,503,340	$16,536,741
Year 30	$0	1,653,674	$18,190,415
Total Saved	$1,250,000		

with your $400,000 per year. I am happy to do a Lifestyle Plan with you. Tell me when you have read the book from cover to cover and I will do it for free!

Now, with the other $350,000, you are going to take steps to get all set up for a fun life in years 7-30. Remember, this is an example. Go to our website www.financialdevelopment.org and use the tools to calculate your numbers exactly; alternatively, give us a call and we will help you.

The following represents what your income could look like during your lifetime. Notice you are depositing money the first seven years, and then you are withdrawing every year for the next 23 years. This is money you can draw on without working. This is income you have already earned and saved. Anything you do to create more income is just a juicy topping on what you set aside in those first seven years!

	Deposit	Interest Earned	Account Balance
Year 1	$350,000	35,000	$385,000
Year 2	$350,000	73,500	$808,500
Year 3	$350,000	115,850	$1,274,350
Year 4	$350,000	162,435	$1,786,785
Year 5	$350,000	213,679	$2,350,464
Year 6	$350,000	270,046	$2,970,510
Year 7	$350,000	332,051	$3,652,561
Year 8	($370,000)	328,256	$3,610,817
Year 9	($370,000)	324,082	$3,564,899
Year 10	($370,000)	319,490	$3,514,388
Year 11	($370,000)	314,439	$3,458,827
Year 12	($370,000)	308,883	$3,397,710
Year 13	($370,000)	302,771	$3,330,481
Year 14	($370,000)	296,048	$3,256,529

Year 15	($370,000)	288,653	$3,175,182
Year 16	($370,000)	280,518	$3,085,700
Year 17	($370,000)	271,570	$2,987,270
Year 18	($370,000)	261,727	$2,878,997
Year 19	($370,000)	250,900	$2,759,897
Year 20	($370,000)	238,990	$2,628,887
Year 21	($370,000)	225,889	$2,484,775
Year 22	($370,000)	211,478	$2,326,253
Year 23	($370,000)	195,625	$2,151,878
Year 24	($370,000)	178,188	$1,960,066
Year 25	($370,000)	159,007	$1,749,073
Year 26	($370,000)	137,907	$1,516,980
Year 27	($370,000)	114,698	$1,261,678
Year 28	($370,000)	89,168	$980,846
Year 29	($370,000)	61,085	$671,930
Year 30	($370,000)	30,193	$332,123
Total Saved	($6,060,000)		

In this example, you put in $350,000 for 7 years, and withdraw $370,000 for the next 23 years. In the end, you have $332,123 left over to spend as you please. You have effectively pulled out $6,060,000 more than you deposited into the account, all from the labor of your little soldiers earning interest for you. When you are at year 30 you can start taking those interest only payments from your long term plan and really start living it up with your almost $2,000,000 per year income.

***Structured correctly, a large part of that
$1,800,000 per year could also be tax-free!***

◇◇◇◇◇◇◇◇◇◇◇◇◇◇

See the *Safety Net* chapter for more details on this. Please understand we are simplifying these examples, but changes in interest rates, investment performance, and transaction fees are necessary to get a more accurate account of your fund growth. This, however, gives you a clear picture of what is possible. Also keep in mind if you earn more, you can live it up a little larger and increase these numbers. Take a few minutes to play with our income calculator at www.financialdevelopment.org to get numbers that match your unique situation.

Crafting Your Future.

It is natural to be less than confident about your future, and to ponder, *Can I really save that much?*

How hard is it to save 10%, 20%, or even 50%? What many people in your situation will do is get paid, live it up, go into debt to purchase far more than they have the earning capacity to cover, and hope they can figure it all out when the money source runs dry. That is not you; you are too smart for that! Saving 10%, 20%, or even 60% of your income does not have to be hard. It will be very difficult, however, if you start off spending first and then try to pull things back after you have established a luxury lifestyle. It is easy to expand; it's often difficult to contract. Just ask anyone who once had it all and has lost it, they will tell you, this type of pain is way worse than never having the money at all!

If you get accustomed to spending $1,000,000 per year, you will find it very difficult to pull back to $400,000 annual spending. However, if you start from the beginning, $400,000 feels like a healthy expansion. People spend what they earn; it is human nature.

What you don't see is easy to save.
What you do see is easy to spend.

◇◇◇◇◇◇◇◇◇◇◇◇◇◇

If you have already started a spending pattern and want to change it, you can. It just takes a whole lot more diligence and can feel a lot more like work than if you start early. If you haven't developed any heavy spending patterns yet, let's start now and keep you on track from day one. If you already have a history of spending all your money, get to our office now so you can get on track without feeling like you are taking everything away from yourself.

Ask any family who is searching for a way to save just 10% of their income. If they have never created a savings program, they will be quite challenged to pull a healthy percentage from their monthly spending plan. I have worked with some people who were limited to saving as their income increases, starting at 2% saved and working up to 10-20% over a few years. However, because you are earning a large part of your lifetime earnings now, it is imperative you get you on the right plan at lightening speed.

> *Wherever you are now, let's get*
> *you started on the right path.*

◇◇◇◇◇◇◇◇◇◇◇◇◇

As you go through the principles in this book, keep in mind we are here to guide and help you; your success is our success. We have made it our mission to have no less than 1,000 athletes living the pro life from draft to old age. Will you be one of our 1,000? Let these numbers be your wake up call. You can have it all—as long as you don't "eat" it all at once.

Chapter 3

LIFE AFTER THE GAME

**How to Choose Your Next Venture
After the Game is Over**

AS YOU GO into your game, you will probably think a lot about what it's going to be like after the game and for right reasons, you are solely focused on making this game the best game you've ever had. Consider this as a truly great analogy about what is happening right now, and why it's so successful. At the same time, you've got to be prepared to choose the next adventure; the next steps you're going to take. What happens when the lights go out, when the game is over, and when retirement comes?

These are the kind of things that often too many athletes don't think about until they are on time's doorsteps, an injury happens suddenly, or they've just started thinking about retirement and have to quickly start building something to step into their retirement. You're in a unique position now because you can think ahead. You're coming in to the league, you've got some good years ahead of you and although it's probably tempting not to worry or think much about what your future's going to be… you owe it to yourself to talk for a little while about what you're going to do after the lights go out.

I often like to start with a "Let's start with the end in mind" conversation with my clients to get them really connected with their overall life purpose. Right now, it might be hard to see anything beyond your sports as your purpose, thinking, *I'm in my purpose right now.* And you are for this moment. But a wise friend of mine taught me that your life purpose, that big thing—the reason you're on the planet—you're born with it and you live with it your entire life; it doesn't change. However, how it manifests in your life does change. And if that's the case then you must have a much bigger purpose. I know it's hard to think past a bigger purpose than this singular moment in time. *I've reached my lifelong goals. I made the Big Time. I've done something that very few people in this world get to ever do, so how can there be a purpose bigger than this?*

Trust me on this one! Once the games are over, you're going to find you really do have a much bigger purpose. The ability to fully fulfill that purpose is going to come based on the planning you put in to play now.

Let's talk about how you get connected to your life purpose. Perhaps you are one of those players fortunate enough to already know exactly what that purpose is:

- You know exactly where you're going.
- You know where your life is headed.
- You know what you want to do with your money.

Congratulations! Unfortunately, far too few people truly understand their life purpose at this stage in the game. So they search, or don't, and sometimes it comes in and shows them what it is; other times they have to really look.

One of the best pieces of advice I ever received was from one of my mentors, Brian Tracy. His words still ring in my ears whenever I feel uncertain of my path, "You know your life purpose from the time you're really young." As I listened to his message, what I learned from it was that we don't come to life and then figure it out; we come in knowing our purpose. Then as time goes on, others influence us; e grow up and learn from our peers, parents, siblings and other family members, and begin to lose focus of what that real purpose is.

Tracy taught me that we recognize our purpose between ages 7 and 14 years old. When I first heard this, I thought it was crazy. What do you mean I knew what my entire life purpose was at 7? Looking back at even 4 or 8 or 10, or definitely before I was even a teenager, how could I have known my life purpose? I questioned it and at first wanted to dismiss it, but what I found was when I gave it a chance and really listened, I realized I had known what I wanted to do and acted it out from the time I was a very small child, around six or seven. I can't help being a teacher!

I've tried to do a lot of things in my life… I'm an entrepreneur who's always looking for the next thing to make life better and make the lives of those around me better, but it always comes back to teaching. In fact, the teacher in me is why I'm helping others like you now—the teacher in me can't stop teaching. I am so committed to sharing wisdom, and it's such a natural part of who I am that it inspired my writing this book in my quest to expand my teaching profession and help others in an area of my greatest expertise.

It just so happens the area where I can claim an expert status is about money and I've had a unique set of experiences, which directed me to a level of knowledge where I can help pro-athletes with their money. But helping pro-athletes is not my life purpose; it's simply the manifestation of my purpose, which happens to be teaching. I am here to be a shining light and spread love on to the planet.

I got a clear revelation of my purpose a few years ago when sitting inside a church that I was visiting from out of town; a church that drew me inside where I just sat and meditated. All of a sudden it was revealed to me that years before my life purpose had been shown to me and strangely it was centered on a vessel I had created. As I recall, I don't know what possessed me to take a pottery class in the middle of my teaching career and to become a student again and learn something new, but I did. I went into the pottery class and gave it my all. It was a hand building pottery class and I created this vase... from scratch. I took piles of lifeless clay, and formed it into a beautifully molded piece. I was so surprised that it actually turned out exactly how I wanted it to. It amazed me because I'm not that artistic and didn't really think I could do it, but I'm so proud of the accomplishment it's actually my prized piece today.

The point is not really that the vase itself showed me my purpose— no, it was that I kept feeling drawn to pray and seek while I was creating this vase. The whole time I was creating it, I kept saying over and over, God, help me be the vessel that can stay so full of your love that I can overflow it to everyone who comes near me; that I can overflow onto everyone who ever comes into my presence. If I can just stay full of your love, I can bless others by just being myself.

I didn't realize while I was making the vase that eight years later I would sit in a church in a city I was visiting and the experience would come back to me and clearly show me my life purpose. But it did show up: as a six-year-old, a seven-year-old, and an eight-year-old; I was a born leader. I was the one who always rushed in to make everybody else feel better. I would teach them exactly what they needed to know. I never really did much for them; I always made them learn to do for themselves.

Even as a young girl, when I helped my friends with homework or I helped a friend with a problem, I was never one to solve the problem for them. Instead, I would sit down and show them how they could solve the problem, instinctively knowing they would then be able to solve that problem every time they faced it… I understood this from a young age.

Now, what does my story have to do with your life purpose? It's simply this. If you're not sure what your life purpose is and if you're not sure why you're on this planet, if you're really not sure what the big picture is or maybe it's piled underneath the sea of lights and fans and parties and all the fun parts that come with being a pro-athlete, don't worry. All you have to do is take a moment, remember what you loved to do when you were a kid. It may not show up for you right away and that's okay. Just start thinking, *What was it that I loved to do. How did I show up no matter what I was playing?* No matter what you were doing, what is the consistent thing that you always did? You always were? Even if all you ever thought about was sports, how did you show up as you played? Once you start asking yourself these questions, you're going to start to notice a pattern. You might not get the result in one time of asking the questions; it might take several tries. It might take going through the process and just staying open to the answer and one day, all of a sudden, there it will be! You will realize, *this is who I really am at the core. Take out all of the bells and whistles and this is who/what I really am.*

When I realized I was a teacher, I was shocked! I did not think of myself as a teacher. I was not comfortable teaching little kids; it just didn't make sense to me. I my mind, I knew teachers taught little kids, but I stumbled into a college classroom at the age of 23, began teaching and never looked back. Who would have known?

And as you search for your own life purpose, give yourself a break. Relax. You're doing great. In fact, you're probably more connected to your life purpose than you think, and I can bet you that somehow, part of that connection shows up in what you're doing now. Again, remember what my friend taught us, Whatever you're doing now is the manifestation of your life purpose. Now is the time to look around and discover:

- How do you show up on the team?
- What's that key factor that all the other players seem to notice about you?
- What makes you different or sets you apart?

These are likely clues into what your overall life purpose is. You're just seeing how they manifest out on the field or on the court. Identifying your life purpose doesn't have to be something you get overnight so don't worry if it doesn't come, if you're struggling, or if you feel frustrated because you just haven't been able to master it yet. Relax into it and know that you have plenty of time to figure it out because whatever you're doing, you're already—at some level—living your life purpose. In everything that you do, it's going to show up. The question is, how can the life purpose you discover help you to plan what is the next thing you want to do when the games are over?

Understanding The Power of Your Position.

As a pro-athlete, you're in a very unique position, one that many people in the world will never experience. Many of us struggle, starting from zero. We work hard, we build up, and we finally at some point reach a level of income that supports the goals and the dreams that we have for our lives.

In fact, did you know most people don't reach their peak income until around the age of 55? If most people peak their income at the age of 55, then that means that they work almost their entire lives to arrive at that point.

Set Yourself Up For Long Term Success.

As you move closer to your life purpose and start to embrace the power you hold right now in having the income and the resources available to do what you want, let's review some ways that you can set yourself up for long-term success.

There are **three main areas you can improve in your life right now**, which will make a difference when you're ready to step out of the game and do what you want to do next. The first thing you want to focus on is building the skills now that allow you to do what you want to do later. For instance, if you know you want to coach young children, start thinking about how they relate, and how you will interact with young children. Spend more time with nieces and nephews, or maybe your own children. Also, consider volunteering: be a big brother, a big sister, or something similar that works with your schedule.

You can start building the skills right now for what you want to do later. If you know you want to be a public speaker and you want to motivate people and show them how they can become anything they want to be, then you could practice speaking. Get in front of your teammates and deliver motivational speeches to them. Go to your family: be motivational when you speak to them. Volunteer at local organizations; offer to speak to a college classroom or groups, a rotary club, maybe a Chamber of Commerce. You can start doing these things and building these skills right now; each volunteer effort builds the skills to allow you to participate in whatever you want to do in the future. You will be fascinated that in most cases, you tend to navigate into the things you're good at anyway. If you really know you want to do something specific—start building the necessary skills— and it will be a natural progression for you to draw on those skills when you exit the game.

Use your off-season time to prepare for the next phase of your life.

◇◇◇◇◇◇◇◇◇◇◇◇◇

Another area you want to think about while you are still playing is to build relationships and partnerships that will help take you where you want to be. If you know you want to work on Wall Street or you want to be involved with an organization, go there. Start building relationships now. Ask the famous question: "How can I be of service?" It seems a little bit tough, right? Sometimes you want to go in and see what you can get from someone, but simply asking the question, "How can I be of service?" will open far more doors to you and create valuable relationships.

In today's world, relationships are the primary power through which you achieve your goals. If you want to work on Wall Street, you have to be involved: learn more about it, join with the brokers, and connect with people who are working on Wall Street. They don't have to be doing exactly what you want to do, but the closer they are to the work you want to be doing, the better. And more importantly, the closer they are to the people who hire or train or invite others to that work, even better. Create powerful partnerships. You're in a unique position to go straight to the top and be heard. You don't have to climb the ladder and you don't have to beg and plead for a meeting with the CEO. The CEO's simply hear you want to speak with them and knowing your position as a pro-athlete, they're very likely to say, "Hey there could be a partnership here." There could be a deal. They start to think, *hmm, this could really be good for me.*

The decision makers start saying yes to you, often as soon as they know you're willing to speak to them. They're probably really excited and might even put on their best suit, get a fresh haircut and bring extra staff to make sure that they impress you! How cool is that?

Build those relationships; make yourself available. Create friendships and partnerships. Get to know the people who are doing what you want to do. If you want to move into the motivational speaking industry as we discussed before, just as you would be practicing on-the-field skills, you will want to build skills in developing relationships. Ask the right questions:

- Who can get me on these stages?
- Who can book me to speak?
- Who would put me on their stage?
- What do I have to offer?
- Do I want to speak in the university circuit, or do I want to speak at motivational seminars?
- Is Tony Robbins your hero; do you want to focus on someday speaking for him? Get to know him.

Again, you're in a unique position that these opportunities are very possible for you, so go for it. Build those relationships now; be a friend—be a confidant. You may even find those relationships start to help you and support you in many other areas besides the ones that you're specifically going for in the long term.

The third way that you can really set yourself up for success in the long term is by taking mini trials to test the ideas you have now, which you want to do later. Let's take a motivational speaker example. Later in your life you may want to be a motivational speaker. After the game is done, you've made your money and you've planned well and you don't really have to work... there may still be a drive in you to give back or conquer the next great idea. Motivational speaking may be the path for you, or so you think right now. There's a way to take a deeper dive long before you have to enter that field and make it your focus, only to find out you've put an extra level of energy and effort into something that maybe you don't even like doing.

Motivational speakers travel often. You've been travelling with your team, do you want to keep travelling? Maybe that works for you or maybe you'd just like to find a place and settle down in one city and stay there. These are the kind of things that you must consider. Being in practice and actually doing the things that you want to do are great ways to decide, Is this for me? So if you want to be a motivational speaker, try it out and go do it during the off-season. We've talked about building your skills, but there's a more important piece to a career path than just building a skill. Take advantage of completing a mini trial.

You have the perfect opportunity to do something that you think you want to do, go for it, see what happens and answer so many questions:

- Do you love it?
- Do you hate it?
- Is it just mediocre?
- Do you feel like there's something missing?

Is it possible that what you think you want to do is not a perfect fit for your skill set? You can work on that; build on your skills and once you have them polished, you can then address that you may then feel, Well, it's still lacking luster for me. I'm just not excited. If that's the case, then you know not to pursue that area when you finish your career in the game. I've seen way too many athletes default into work because they are good at it only to find out they hate it. Find out now!

So let's think about other areas that might be beneficial to you in terms of mini trials so you can know if you love your choice or not. Another question you can answer is, Does this provide the level of income that I want to sustain the lifestyle that I've set? In many cases, you might be in a unique situation that you don't need more income and

- Is it going to require time, energy and effort?
- Do you have your time budgeted out so you're able to make time to plan for this new venture?
- Is the timeline here? Now?

Do you know when you'll launch into your plan? It doesn't have to be this year, next year or the year after. It could be a year after finishing your athletic career. It could be within two years of planning to retire. Whatever the relative time is for you, plan that out. Know when you want to get started; the best time to start may be now.

You've discovered how to set yourself up for success in the long term; it doesn't have to require a lot. Just make sure that you're doing something and that you're clear about the direction you're going. And hey, if it changes along the way, the best part is once you've done it one time, it's really not hard to create the plan again for a different opportunity. Trust me; I've done my share of planning for the *next thing* in my life trying to figure out exactly where I should be and what is the best market for me to serve with my skills and talents and with my big heart.

Let's Plan Your Next Venture

I've included some worksheets for you to use; they can be found on our website:

www.financialdevelopment.org

Download the full PDF of the workbook. It includes all the worksheets mentioned in this book. They will help you really get clear and plan your next great venture.

You've got this! You are a superstar and you can stay a superstar your entire life if that's what you want. Let's do it. Let's plan your next venture.

Chapter 4

FAMILY INVOLVEMENT

WHEN IT COMES to money, there is one thing that can make us go broke faster than any other: family. I would suspect not many of you have families you want to attribute to this, but it is the truth far too often. Our families do not intend to help us go broke; they just know how to push our buttons better than anyone else. You love them. You feel sorry for them. You want to help them all.

The truth is, if you try to take what you are earning and help your entire family without proper planning, you will all end up in the poor house. That is where a powerful and purposeful system comes into place so you are able to take care of your family the way you want to, but in a way that supports them—and you—now and for years to come. When it comes to family, there are **three key areas** that can lead to more success for everyone.

1. Keep your family involved in your decision process so they understand the decisions you make.
2. Set clear boundaries and teach them exactly what is and is not acceptable to you.
3. Create clear expectations of what your *Big Time* means for them and what you need from them to make this work.

Let's look first at keeping your family involved.

When you first hit the big success status, you notice very quickly that you have cousins, aunts, uncles, distant family members, friends, and all kinds of people suddenly claiming you who may not have given you the time of day before. They weren't there in the gym when you were working hard at practice, training harder at 5 o'clock in the morning, and munching on meat and veggies while every one else enjoyed grandma's famous mashed potatoes. I am going to be blunt here! These people do not deserve a dime from you. It is not how much they need your help that matters here. It is what they deserve by how they have been there for you when you weren't on top of the world.

Who was supporting you?

Who was there cheering you on, taking you to practice before you could drive, waiting up for you to make sure you didn't forget to eat?

These are the family members I am talking about. These are the people who deserve for you to keep them in the loop and ultimately help them understand your plan and how you are creating lifetime success for all of you.

> *Notice I didn't say they deserve your money,*
> *just that they deserve to understand what you are up to.*

◇◇◇◇◇◇◇◇◇◇◇◇◇◇

You will learn later in this chapter about how to be smart about helping out deserving family members. First, let's look at what it means to keep them informed. This simply means you get your plan together and share with them what you are doing, and why they can't be rolling in Bentley's right now, even though you have enough money to buy them one. It is all about making decisions here, and these are your decisions to make. Explain your plan if you must.

If you have not yet made an appointment with a financial strategist, do so. Call our office and we will be happy to set you up with a plan. This is one of the key elements in communicating. You have to know and understand what you are doing yourself before you can share it with your family. Once you have a clear plan, share that with the family members you love and who deserve to know what's up.

Get your financial strategist involved; ask them to share with your family exactly how what you are doing now will help all of you in the future. If you are in a situation where you must help some of your family now, like parents, guardians, siblings, and other really close relatives, weigh out how much help they really need, and make them sit down with your financial strategist so you can help them manage money better too.

Your commitment to your family is important, and we get it. This is why we have created our business model around supporting your desire to help your family. Our *Family Success Program* specifically targets teaching your family how to be most supportive of your goals. And if you desire to help them financially, when it is time for you to turn over some money to them we have an entire process dedicated to help you save thousands in taxes and educate them so it truly helps them now and in the future. Our mission is to help your family become self sufficient and no longer need to reach to you for handouts once you help them one time. More on this later...

You will be surprised what just a little bit of open communication about your plan can do to get your family on your side and supporting your decisions to give or not to give to them right now. Keep in mind, though, that sometimes they really may not quite get it. They may feel like you should just solve their problems now and may even call you selfish. You have got to learn to be ok with not being appreciated by all those you love who may not understand your plan. The pressure can be real; be ready.

Setting Boundaries.

When it comes to helping family, you have to get really good at finding out how much of that need they show you suddenly shows up just because they know you have money and how much of their struggle is real. Be sure you are *supporting* them to get to a better place and not *enabling* them to do nothing to improve their lives while you take care of them. The key is to courageously set clear and consistent boundaries.

Think of your situation like coaching your family to success. For example, if your coaches took you out of conditioning practice and let you sit until you caught your breath, would you be the athlete you are today? No. They pushed you. Sometimes they even pushed you until you threw up. And you kept going, didn't you? Sometimes you have to be like the tough coach who lets those you care about go through a little bit of a rough time so they, too, can get better.

> *In order to make sure your Big Time lasts a lifetime,*
> *you are going to have to make some tough decisions.*

◇◇◇◇◇◇◇◇◇◇◇◇◇

To be clear, I am not here to step between anyone and his desire to take care of his momma. I am here, however, to make sure you can take care of momma for life if that is what you want to do. Those tough decisions sometimes mean you are going to have to say No to people you really care about. Keep in mind, this is often just for a *season* so you can set yourself up, but it will be worth it when you know your future is set and you can afford to be generous forever and not only today.

Setting boundaries with your families can be one of the toughest things you go through in your development of relationships. Far too often, they will not understand your decisions and you will get marked within your family as selfish, greedy, heartless, stingy, snobby—and many other not so nice names—as they look to justify why you may not be making it rain happy money all through the family. You have got to get good at ignoring this negativity and emotional pressure and love them anyway while you work to understand this is *your* journey and it is not their job to understand or control it. You can choose to stay away, or you can choose to go ahead and stay close with your family—knowing you may have to deal with it is just a new dynamic now.

Whatever you choose, know that you are choosing the right thing for you and your family in the long run by having and sticking to a clear financial plan. And yes, you've hit it big, so save back a few dollars and have some fun once in a while. Treat them well. I don't suggest you be stingy at all; give and have fun, but set the amount of your giving in advance so you know what you can do without messing up your long-term plan.

It may feel like I am being a little harsh here suggesting you hold out on those you love. I know what it is like to advance beyond the ranks of your family and have them call you snooty, stingy, rich, and many other things. I want to share with you some of my own story so you know what I suggest to you I have also done myself.

I was born to a lower middle class family in a small town. My mother gave me up to be adopted by my grandparents. She was and is still in my life, but I had a set of parents I call mom and dad, who are my grandparents by birth. As I recall, I never knew we were essentially poor.

I seemed to have everything I needed. When it came time for dances, I had a dress. Once a year we would drive to the Smokey Mountains and have a vacation. I never really even gave money a thought.

Then there came a time when my dad, a dedicated pastor to a not so thriving church, had to make a decision. We could no longer afford to keep our home and to keep the church going. He carried most of the church bills. His decision was to save the church, so we gave up our home and moved into the basement of the church. For the first time in my life I experienced lack.

It was then, at age 14, life set in motion a determination in me to never be poor when I grew up and to never have to go through that kind of trauma again. I was embarrassed, ashamed, and even stopped hanging out with my friends because I didn't think they would like me now that I lived in a church because I was so poor. I didn't have the understanding then that I have now; all I knew was I felt shame. I gained a ton of weight for a 14-year old—15 pounds. I had more than my fair share of the brownies we sold out of our home to make extra money. Looking back it doesn't seem so horrible, but at the time I was devastated.

Coming from this place, I grew up, went to college, and because I was getting married young, decided I better take a personal finance course. That one course showed me I do have the power to control my life and how money shows up in it, so I studied anything and everything to do with money; finance accounting, and economics. I married into what some people might consider decent money—his family, not my husband—but he was a big spender so we always had to depend on his parents to stay afloat. It seemed I had family members all the time looking for a handout, but I could hide behind my husband who was very stingy anyway and ultimately they simply stopped asking because he primarily said, No.

When it got tricky was when I finally decided at the age of 30 to divorce him. It was a scary and painful decision, but it was one I needed to make. I did it, and set out to grow my own income so I could sustain the lifestyle I desired for my two boys. Within 18 months, I had not only matched the dual income we had earned as a couple. I had exceeded it! I was earning over six figures for the first time in my life, and it felt great! I had to work all the time back then to make it happen, but I was doing it.

So why was this a problem? All of a sudden, I didn't have anyone else to hide behind when my family came after me needing help. I helped them some, but of course it was the same ones who seemed to need help all the time. There came a point where I had to just say No. Guess what! I became the one who was snobby, stingy, and selfish in the eyes of some of my family members. They would get mad at me and say I didn't care about them or didn't love them. All the time for a period of time, their main connection to me was to ask for favors, monetary and otherwise.

Here is the part where you should really listen!

◇◇◇◇◇◇◇◇◇◇◇◇◇

Eventually, they just stopped asking. They already knew the answer was going to be No so they didn't ask anymore. They stopped calling me greedy and selfish and just started interacting with me like normal family again. It took a while, but we did get there. I would get the occasional remark that I thought I was rich, which I guess I was compared to those around me. But at some point we were able to be normal like family again.

One of the ways I did help out my family, if you are looking for a way to find balance, was to hire them to do all kinds of things for me. I have always been an entrepreneur in addition to my classroom teaching, so I always had some kind of work they could do for me. I also owned my own house so I would hire them to clean, mow the lawn, and other tasks.

This part can be tricky because not all family members can be trusted to actually do the work. I kept hiring those who did it right, and I stopped hiring those who didn't. I treated it like I was hiring anyone else. Be careful of this tactic, but if it works for you, it is a great way to help the family out without giving to the point of perpetuating their neediness.

In the middle of all this, I let my birth mother sit at the jailhouse because she was associating with the wrong people. I have told some of my family I would not help them even when I had the money, and I even had to call the Sheriff to evict my brother out of my home in Ohio while I was living in Florida because he snuck in and was staying there with several of his drug addict friends. Oh, yes! That one made my birth mom really mad at me.

You've got to choose who and when you help; family and friends alike. If you allow them to use you, they will. Some of my family members have been amazing and supportive of my journey, and even worked for me and during tighter times waited to get paid when I could afford it. Those are the ones I like to take care of now. The takers just have to go look somewhere else to get their needs met.

I set solid boundaries; I am not willing not participate or assist anyone who would use my support to continue a drug problem or a lifestyle I do not agree with. I love them and will continue to love them… I just choose not to get involved. It wasn't always that way.

**_Setting boundaries is a skill you must develop
over time. It does eventually get easier._**

◇◇◇◇◇◇◇◇◇◇◇◇◇

I share this with you not to pretend I am a hard ass who doesn't care. In fact, many times I have been very sad over these situations. However, I want you to see that sometimes even when it is your own family you must set boundaries in order to support your own values and your own goals. You cannot expect your entire family to naturally support your boundaries. These lines are your own responsibility to set. If you hold firm to them long enough you will find that eventually it does get easier. Then you may be able to help out in ways that can bless your family without setting an expectation you don't want to or cannot continue to meet.

Setting Clear Expectations.

Create clear expectations of what your *Big Time* means for your family and what you need from them to make this work. When your family has been with you along the journey to your success, it is no surprise when they feel like they should also share in your glory. For those family members, you may want to keep them close, take care of them, and be sure you honor their part in the long journey and hard work you have put in to get here.

Doing so can be a very joyful time. However, if you do not set clear expectations about what it means now that you have become successful, to bring your family along can become stressful instead of joyful. The same goes for yourself, actually. If you do not set clear expectations for what your athletic success means for you financially, you will stress yourself out, too. This is where getting clear and setting clear expectations can make or break the way you feel in your everyday life.

What Does It Mean To Set Clear Expectations?

There are several areas to improve your life for which you can use these techniques, but we are going to focus here on what it means to set clear financial expectations. Clear expectations must first be set for yourself.

First, you must take a look at what has been established as your overall goal. This is the big picture view that includes what you want your life to look like in 3 months, 6 months, a year, 2 years, 10 years, was their fault; based on the requirements I had established, I couldn't give them money right then. Yes, they started leaving me alone. And if you are wondering, yes I did this to my own brother. To this day, he no longer asks me for money.

What if you can't say, No? Find someone who can hold you accountable and let the boundaries you set say, No for you. For instance, one of the services we offer our clients is Social Mitigation. This is a custom service as needed, but as one example, we simply set up the guidelines with our athletes and when their family and friends come asking for money, they can respond, I run all of my spending through my financial strategist, so you will have to show a case for how this is necessary and will help all of us and I will take it to their office and see if we can get this approved. While the athlete holds full decision-making power for final decisions, we help mitigate the asks and give the players an easy-out.

While we recommend first learning to hold your own ground, this is helpful for young athletes whose parents are the ones pushing them for requests that could ultimately create financial failure. It comes down to this, if you can't say No to mom, let us—or your chosen financial strategist—do it for you.

Chapter 5

ENJOYING YOUR MONEY NOW AND LATER

WHEN YOU THINK about saving, most of the time the first thing that comes to mind is, *I have to give up something. What are you going to take from me now so that I can have a future later?* The idea is just not very appealing, is it? I don't like it either.

The thing is… when you plan your future, it's more important to really examine what you truly want in life and inquire how the decisions that you're making now help you get there.

In a recent conversation with my (then) four-year-old niece, she asked me, Aunt Crystal, I talk too much, don't I? I ask way too many questions.

I said, Actually, Brylee, questions are what make us smarter. If you didn't ask questions, how would you ever know the answers?

for that game, or cut some. Ok then, there is a process to cut some fat: you start to measure and pay close attention.

You look at the labels of your food and if you're counting calories to gain or lose weight before weigh-ins, you even look at the calories in all the food. When you first start, you have to stop and consider all these things because you don't know the information, but as you continue to move forward, you realize all you already know. You've looked it up numerous times and you know by memory approximately how many calories, how much fat, and how many carbs are in that slice of bread or piece of steak and what impact it will have on your goals.

Once you've tracked information long enough, you don't have to go back and look at the data anymore. You simply track it in your mind as your knowledge grows. Maybe you do jot it down and continue to keep track, but you don't have to look it up anymore. You can start to use our calculator to just ask, Well, if I make this purchase, what's the future value of the purchase that I could have toward some other *goal* I have in the future?

You start to easily make those judgments so that for instance, every time you do go for a Starbucks, you can actually think, *What I'm giving up for this Starbucks is not the $4.25 or the $5.75 but it's the future value of the money represented and this is what it will change in my future.* And you can look at the real cost. And it's okay if it turns out that that $4.25 is $12.75 in its long-term value, and you say, You know what, it's worth $12.75 to have this Starbucks because I just enjoy the face of the beautiful woman who serves it to me with a smile that makes me feel like I'm a real person! You never know. That might be a $12.75 value interaction for you. So go for it. Just know that it's a $12.75 interaction and not a $4.25 exchange.

When you start to think about enjoying your money now, the first piece of that is really about having a balance between spending and saving. The questions will run through your mind: How much do I save?

How much do I spend? How much is it okay for me to spend? Well, the truth is, it's your money, so it's completely okay if you spend it all.

The problem with spending it all today is the expenditure may not be okay to the future version of you.

There is a you who is waiting, knowing you have completed the work that allows you to relax a little bit and enjoy your future life in a different way. Life and money really requires a balance, and it's up to you to decide how – and how much. The cool thing is, if you use our calculators, you can actually take a look at what you want your lifestyle to be, how you want to be included in that, where you want to live, and what kind of activities you want to enjoy. You can literally take into account all these things so that when you're making *spend-save* decisions, you will already know the answer to your questions:

- Do I have enough saved?
- Do I have enough to spend on this item?

You will have created a spending plan. If you don't want to think about it every single time, then you can make it as simple as knowing, I've already done the work; I know how much I need for the *future version* of myself.

Let's look at a plan that leads you in the right direction. Let's say that you are going to allow yourself $450,000 a year to spend or buy whatever it is that you want. By the way, $450,000 is more than the US president makes. So congratulations, you've now made more than the United States president and you're on a savings plan at the same time. So when you reach the end of the *Big Time*, it's a matter of just looking at your spending plan and staying on track as you think, *Well, I* that meal. Guess what? You've earned it. You have every right to do that.

But… what if you also looked at what would it take to have the meal catered; perhaps your home or another more luxurious place. Maybe the views are spectacular. Maybe you could even find a friend's home… you're running in some nice circles… perhaps you can find a place that provides waterfront dining. Determine how much it would cost to have food catered and bring that meal to you and your family. Gone are the price tags; there's no menu with prices in front of them, making the overall experience more enjoyable for you and your guests. Maybe you even have a place for the little kids who want to come along to go and play. What if the total cost was $1,500 to cater the meal for everyone in a wonderful location that's even better than the swanky restaurant experience? These are examples of how you can make wise choices and still continue to enjoy what you've created with the wealth you earned through your hard work and dedication.

Wise choices are not always labeled with don't!

- Don't feed the family.
- Don't take friends out for a meal.
- Don't reward others.

Absolutely. DO each of these things if they matter to you—particularly if you can actually weigh out the total value of what you're getting against what it actually costs. You might even find that the value could be greater and the cost less. This obviously isn't limited to dinner, but certainly is an example of how you can look and ask, How else can I do this?

Again, let the driving question be the energy that leads you to the right answer to the question, How can I reward my family and friends in the biggest way for the least amount of cost to me? That's a great question to ask. Again, not that you're being cheap; you're just making wise decisions.

Now, here's the proverbial $64,000 question: How do I indulge without going broke? The truth is, the most detrimental piece to most puzzles of anyone's financial picture is they want to indulge but they also want to have the money. Yup! They want to have their cake and eat it, too. Well, here's the cool part: Set up your saving in advance. If you know you've already planned for the future, and you put money away where you can't easily get your hands on it right now, so you can't just go grab it out of the bank, you've already protected yourself from going broke. You've been smart; you've done what you need to do and now it's time to think about indulging. In the last section, we looked at how to allow the indulgences, especially if it could create a more valuable experience. But the question remains, How do you really indulge? Well, there are so many ways to achieve your goals.

One of my favorite examples comes from the book, *Money Mastery*, with Tony Robbins. He writes in this particular publication about how many people want, for instance, a private jet. So you want to go out and buy the private jet? You think it will give you a feeling of significance; you own it, and you get to go wherever, anytime you want. But when you truly calculate the total cost of that private jet, you've got to buy the jet, the fuel, and the staff. You've also got to have a place to put the jet when you're not using it and all the different costs that are associated with owning the jet; it's in the hundreds of millions.

But what if you really just want the private jet experience; you want to indulge and you want to feel the experience of a private jet, but you don't really feel the need to have the total ownership. Maybe the significance of ownership is not what you wanted as much as the experience. Well, when you're ready, and you're actually going to take a trip, hire the private jet. You might find that for much less money, especially depending on how often you're going to fly, you can buy the private jet for the weekend or the day or whatever trip you're taking.

Indulge. Enjoy the experience, but without all of the long-term costs associated with ownership, or incurring the huge liability that comes with owning a private jet and everything else that is a part of the package! I encourage you engage this line of reasoning next time you want to indulge. In fact, if you read Robbins' *Money Mastery*, which I highly recommend, you will discover it also has some great investment tips similar to those we will discuss in the Investments chapter. As a sort of full disclosure, I am not advocating any of the investment advice in the book; I am simply suggesting it as a great resource to learn more about investments so you are well informed.

When you make wise decisions, keep in mind that not everything needs to be as big and as grand as you may originally think is needed for you to feel you have indulged. How many times have you gone to a restaurant, and although you really want the big dessert, you know it's not on your agenda. The fitness goals on which you are focused right now don't afford you to have the 5,000-calorie dessert that everyone else seems to think is okay… because they don't have the same goals as you, right? They don't have the fitness goals perhaps that you have to keep. How could you indulge eating all that sugar? Quite simply; you just let somebody else order the dessert; you take a bite or two and you get to taste and enjoy it, but let's face it, you don't get the tummy ache or the added sugar that you don't need. You indulged! You enjoyed, but you didn't necessarily have to buy the whole piece.

SECTION II
MISTAKES TO AVOID

you don't know any better, you do what they say, which ultimately is not such a good idea.

While I admire your desire to do what someone else suggests and listen to someone who may know more than you, I also encourage you to be aware of who it is that gives you advice and know what rights or credentials they have to do so. What is the foundation for their credibility? What do you need to be aware of, regarding the work they're doing and the experiences they've had? In other words, So what? Who are you to say? Who are you to tell me what to do?

Granted, you want to ask the correct questions in a very nice way, but you certainly want also to know the right answers. You are a prudent person; when someone else encourages you or tells you what to do, you want to know:

- What does that mean?
- What should I expect if I should do that?
- What experience, or credentials do you have to provide me that information?

At the end of the day, you need to know what is in it for you and what gain they have to advise you and lead you in a particular direction. You want to make sure when others provide you advice you know what it is you can expect as a result of following that advice.

Another thing I often see is players who will give someone else far too much authority to make decisions for their future. Again, I encourage you to seek financial counsel and get expert advice, and never simply assume someone else will take care of you so you won't have to be involved. Just who do you want to give authority to make decisions for your future? Do you really want to let someone else have that? It sounds kind of crazy, but I've seen it happen over and over where someone makes a great deal of money and allows someone else to take charge. They sign for you; they make financial decisions for you, and invest your money for you... and only later do you find out what did and didn't work. Unfortunately, the damage has been done, because too many times issues arise from what didn't work.

Then your financial future is at risk because someone else was making all the decisions, and they didn't even have to consult you to do so. Be aware when allowing someone else to make those decisions for you. What you're saying is You know better than I do, and You care about me more than I do. The truth is… no one cares about you like you do and should. Well, maybe your mom, but no one else! So keep in mind, when someone else makes decisions for you, you want to stay involved, understand what's going on, and be the one empowered to make decisions or to at least approve them before any action is taken.

Another huge problem I've seen in the context of giving your power to someone else is assuming there's always going to be more money. The thing is, you can't know there's unlimited access to more money. The contract you have right now is the contract that you *have*, and you have nothing else until you *contract* more. You could plan to stay in the game much longer, or plan to re-sign another contract and make millions more, but you can't safely assume there's always going to be more money. You never know today just what the future will hold.

Don't give up the power to someone else to manage your money, hoping that if it doesn't work out, there'll be more.

◇◇◇◇◇◇◇◇◇◇◇◇

Always assume that this is your last contract, and that you must do with this one what you need to do to set yourself up for the future. Then when the next one comes, awesome… you have a bonus! You reassess and start the plan from that secure moment; never give up your power by *assuming* there's going to be more money down the road.

What you have today is what you have and what you know.

◇◇◇◇◇◇◇◇◇◇◇◇◇

I'm an optimist, so I encourage you to plan and dream big for what could come, but also be aware and plan for **what is right now**.

Another big thought riddled with mistakes is when someone hits the *Big Time*... they landed the big contract: they have large amounts of money, and they assume the money they've earned so far is going to somehow last their whole life. This is perhaps more sad than any other mistake I encounter, because it is a mistake of ignorance—not knowing—that sends them into poverty. While I'm a fan of the idea of dreaming big, I have to tell you that when it comes to planning your financial future, somehow is just not a good plan.

In fact, believing in the somehow usually leads to bankruptcy, failed marriages, and myriad other problems stimulated by financial distress. So never expect that your money will just somehow last. Develop a clear plan, and make sure whoever has authority over your funds, or is guiding you through your plan, explains it to you, and you know exactly why and how the money you have earned thus far is supposed to last your lifetime.

Another big problem that I've seen among players is an assumption the league will take care of you. Yes, the league is there to put in place the best resources, which they know will help you be successful, but the truth remains... the league is a profit entity itself. At the end of the day, it is your responsibility to take care of yourself. The resources leagues have are often wonderful, for instance—the NFL resources, which actually protect players from financial advisors who have little to no experience. In order to be recommended by the league, planners have to have eight years of experience, and also have to carry the credentials to do provide financial services, and then... complete a thorough screening process.

This is wonderful, but the league cannot know for sure the motives of each advisor, even though they've met the credentials. There is no certainty on the part of the league that the advisor is working in your best interest, and is concerned more about you and the fiduciary duties to you, as the player, than their own pocketbook. So that's your job; the league can only go so far.

There is no question it's your job, then, to take the next step, which requires you check out the person you've decided to bring on as a trusted advisor. Pay attention to what they've done for their past clients, who they've helped, what happened, and who's recommending them. There may be other areas where you can recognize trigger points and the red flags—long before you sign on to do business with a particular broker or advisor.

Finally, you want to give some serious think time to one big mistake that happens over, and over, and over, which I call *ballin' like it'll never run out*. One of the biggest dangers in giving away your power is to fall into the habit of making choices that cause you to be haphazard in where your money goes. If you do not think about your actions and exactly what you want, when you want something, and with whom you want it… or you look at everything you ever could imaging doing, without thinking about the future, there is a great likelihood you will find yourself in money trouble. Again, I remind you… although I encourage you to take advantage of the lifestyle made possible because of your success—make sure your choices are filtered with thoughtfulness and awareness.

you would any other. Take the extra time you need to make the decision with a sound mind and not based on emotion. We all know sales people are trained regularly to get you to make a decision while you are in an emotional state. Well, let me tell you... ladies know how to get what they want from their man, too!

Treat your lady well, and shower her with nice gifts, but do so in a way that enhances yours and her overall quality of life... now and in the future. When big purchase decisions come up, take the time to really look at what is best overall.

- If she wants a house, look at the benefits of owning that large home.
- How likely are you to be traded to another team?
- How easy will it be to sell the home if you have to move to another state?
- Would she be moving with you if that happened?

There are so many things to consider here; each involves the kind of decision-making you should be calling up your financial strategist for. Bring her along to your strategy appointments; she may learn even more how to support you in your financial goals.

Overall, it is clear that a romantic relationship adds another layer of thinking and complexity to your financial goals. However, if you communicate openly, have a clear plan, and get your significant other on board with your plan... it can be a much more drama-free adventure. Saddle up. It is going to be a fun ride.

Chapter 8

MISTAKE #3: EVERYTHING WORKS ITSELF OUT

THE THIRD MAJOR mistake, which is all too often made by those who suddenly find themselves surrounded with large amounts of income... to sit back and hope everything works itself out somehow. You found this mentioned previously, but I want to go a little deeper with the general concept. Hoping can be a huge mistake that could cost thousands—or even millions—over your lifetime. One of the biggest problems faced by most Americans is the problem of inaction, which often shows itself in one of three ways:

1. Taking no action at all
2. Leaving your money in the hands of friends and family
3. Wishful thinking, hoping someone else shows up to take care of your financial situation.

Chapter 9

MISTAKE #4:
TRUSTING TOO QUICKLY

ANOTHER BIG MISTAKE that is often made when you've reached the *Big Time* and you have tons of money floating around is that all of a sudden many people come around… and each has a special strategy they guarantee will help you. It might be they are people who have loved you or supported you through the whole process and now is your time to trust and help them. Keep in mind…the truth is that trusting too quickly, compared to anything else, is the number one mistake leading to the biggest and fastest erosion of your wallet.

I'm all about trust and I do believe in building trust and relationships, but when it comes to my money, no one touches it until I know and trust them to do what I need them to do with it! Now, if I have money to spare and I want to take a risk, then I make a calculated risk and quietly think, *Hey, I'm going to see what happens with this person using the excess that I can afford to lose.* What happens as you trust others with a little responsibility, and as you are able to experience reasons to trust the relationship, you can start to move forward and trust them with more of your financial decisions.

One of my favorite lines, when anyone that I don't really know very well, asks something from me—or it's in an area that I really don't know them well enough—is, I have learned that trust takes time; let's build a relationship, where it is earned. Let's face it, without earned trust, you can really only guess and hope. You earn trust through dedication, time and relationship building. It just doesn't happen overnight: it's just not something you can buy from or place or someone. Those interested in serving your financial needs have to earn the privilege.

I encourage you to not trust others too quickly, especially now that you're in the spotlight and you'll experience many people who will reach out and pretend they're helping you, when all they really want is to help themselves.

The first way to know that you're trusting too quickly is if someone is selling a flashy line of BS and you buy it. If the offer smacks of flashy, fun, exciting, get rich quick, do this now, exclusive... keep in mind all these words are great for getting you on board, but are likely bad for your wallet. Be mindful that something that is flashy and fun and exciting is likely disguised for something that is going to take your money directly from your pocket to theirs.

Don't trust anyone who's selling you a flashy line of BS. You won't know that it's BS and they certainly won't tell you, so your BS detector has to come into full play so you can decide and see it for yourself. Pay attention.

Be aware of exclusive words like my favorite... only for you. When you hear the words, This is only for you and only for this moment, take the words as a huge red flag that somebody is trying to take you to the cleaners.

Let's face it, unless they've known you their entire lives, there's nothing most people will do only for you. Good friendships you've built throughout your entire life, yeah, their actions might be only for you. But someone who met you last week, there's not a single thing in this world they're doing only for you. This is a deliberate ploy on your ego; they need to be shown you are smarter than that!

Another area that could create a mistake by trusting too quickly is getting involved in anything presented as for today only. You read about this in the previous section, but make sure you fully understand *today only* means *if you don't take action now,* you might see through my scheme. It's probably not really that great a deal, and possibly not in your best interest at all. He who pushes this kind of deal will probably try to get you to sign right now and make it official; unfortunately, by the time you know it's no good, you've already signed and the deal is done. I reiterate, today only is another line of flashy BS.

Another thing you might often do—and I personally tend to do same—is to assume everyone advising you has your best interest in mind. Especially if you automatically care about the well-being of others, it's easy to assume that everyone else cares about your well-being. It is natural to think other people are like you; it's just a natural human response. But once you've reached the status you now have, there are way more people who are here, ready and willing to pretend they are concerned for you, when they're really concerned about their wallet. Let's face it, very few people do anything as purely selfless acts. You might do some things where the reason you're doing it serves a bigger cause, but you have to gain from it at some level, even if that gain is nothing more than your own feeling of self worth—knowing you helped someone. There's still some kind of selfish motive, even if it is healthy

For instance, my career is in offering financial education for athletes and families to guide them to beneficial financial strategies. I love helping people; it feeds my soul and it makes me happy, and there's a basic intent to help my clients and grow their wealth that guides my practice. But at the end of the day, if I don't get paid for the services I offer, I wouldn't be doing it. I would have to move to something where I can take care of my own financial future and get paid myself, right? Wouldn't you expect that? Just because you are good at playing ball and you enjoy the game doesn't mean that you would want to give up your paycheck. Keep in mind that while professionals act as fiduciaries for you, they do so for their own good as much as yours. Be aware that this is true, and anyone who tells you they are completely selfless in their efforts are quietly alerting you; look deeply at the raised red flag.

Some may choose to have your best interest in mind, such as someone in a financial practice similar to my own. I choose to the best interest of my clients for many reasons. Number one, it's my fiduciary duty and I've taken an oath to do so but also, I get paid more when I concern myself with your bottom line because ultimately you will refer your friends to me and they will pay me, too. So again, is that really about you? Or is it primarily about me having my own interest in mind—or maybe a healthy combination thereof?

Further, I have a strong sense of personal satisfaction when my work changes the lives of athletes and their families for good. Undergirding all my good work, it is the innate sense of value and accomplishment that keeps me going. Look for people who are honest and willing to tell you, Hey, I have something to gain in this relationship, too. Otherwise, why would anyone enter into a relationship with you if they don't have something to gain? Look for honesty and integrity first, before you consider building a relationship where they can earn your trust and become part of an inner circle of advisory to you. It is ok to have self-driven motives, as long as these motives equally support the needs and goals of those you serve.

When you hit the *Big Time,* all of sudden you've got cousins that you never knew you had— and friends who remember you from high

1. It will make you more money due to an increase in value—we call this appreciation.
2. It will bring you a stream of income that is higher than the costs you have to pay out in order to get that income.

If you stick to this one rule and require that every use of debt matches one of these two considerations, you avoid a potential financial mess and join the ranks of the 78% of NFL players and the 60% of NBA who go broke within two to five years of leaving the game.

Drinks On Me

Now let's talk about generosity. I encourage generosity and believe you are blessed when you bless others with your abundance. However, when you get caught up in being the cool guy and paying for everything for those around you, the risk, once again, is stealing from your *future-self*. It is critical to remember the point made earlier that as a pro-athlete you are earning the majority of your lifetime income in a few short years. While you have more money than most of your friends and family today, if you do not protect it, who will be there to buy you drinks once your career is finished? Buying rounds of drinks every night and living the high life, surrounded by all those who are very happy to bask in your joy with you as long as you get the tab, could be detrimental to your financial future. If you are using a credit card to be the guy who picks up the tab, this makes matters even worse. The same principles apply to other areas, including gambling.

The easiest way to avoid being generous to a fault is to take only cash with you when you head to big social events. Doing so allows you to decide before you begin the night just how much you are willing to spend. Then when you are out with your friends and want to take care of them because of your big heart, you have predetermined how much generosity you have the luxury for that night. More importantly, as the drinks take you another shot deeper than your reason can handle, you easily limit potential drunken losses to the cash in your pocket and save your friends from a massive hangover. Everybody wins.

Strategic tip: Have your bank set a low daily limit on a credit card and use only that one to go out.

Competitive Spending

Another issue that often trips you up when you have plenty of money to spend is the idea that because your peers have something you must also have it. This is popularly called keeping up with the Joneses and often leads to more trouble than other areas of financial decision making, because it feels safe and seems logical. If everyone else is doing it, it must be ok, right?

Let's keep it real, here. If you had done what everyone else did through high school, college, and beyond, you would not be where you are today. And if you were to do what everyone else is doing around you right now, you would not be reading this book or interested in taking control of your financial future. You are a pro-athlete, and what it took to get here was never normal or everyone would have done it.

So how do you know what is acceptable and what is not? It starts with a clear plan of where you want to go and how you plan to get there. If you have a clear plan, it is easy to decide each and every time you spend money if your choices will help you achieve your goal. This kind of clarity makes such a difference in your wealth status that you will find yourself loving those moments you see everyone else spending… and you choose not to. Have you ever been the sober guy at a drunk party and get a kick out of watching all the crazy drunk people? You will find that same sense of power when you watch your peers spending their money on things they don't need and wouldn't even want if someone else didn't have them!

This Section is going to reveal the best nine strategies you can use to be sure the wealth you create now stays with you later. The strategies are here to save you in taxes, protect what you've earned, help your money grow, and help you build a legacy. I have specifically chosen these specific nine because they build the cornerstones to your overall financial wealth.

They are simple; you can easily follow them, and you do not need to get involved with a tricky investment plan to put them into action. Yes, investments are a part of this plan, but you will notice it is not the only strategy, nor is investing given more emphasis than the other strategies in this section. This is because *your financial wealth is not just about investing*! So many times I have watched players follow the advice of someone who knows about some investment and either lose their money or find themselves unprotected from other unexpected, unfortunate circumstances.

Don't trust anyone who tells you one strategy is all you need. You would not want to follow a coach who ran only one play every time. Keep that same policy in mind as you make decisions about your money.

Chapter 11

STRATEGY #1: START A HOME BASED BUSINESS

ONE KEY STRATEGY you can use to plan your future is to set up a home based business right away. There are so many tax benefits of having a home-based business, and if you choose wisely you could at the same time set up an extra stream of income for your household. The following includes a few key areas to consider when planning a home-based business.

Choosing A Business

When choosing which home-based business you will start, consider these **five key questions.**

1. What do you love doing when you are not practicing or playing games?
2. What is something about which you are passionate?

3. In what areas do you naturally have talent and/or you have developed skills?
4. What are some products or services you have used that you would be proud to share with others (or already do share)?
5. Who do you know who is successfully running a home-based business, who would also be a great mentor for you?

Once you have considered these questions, you are on track to choose the general area of business you would like to start. Keep in mind, this has to be something that can be done part time or with very little effort on your part while you are still at the peak of your athletic career. You want to create something that reduces your taxes now and sets you up for something you can build in the future. If you have a spouse who can start building a business now, this is a great way to really get it started while you focus on your game. If not, then just having it established and working on it during the off-season is enough.

If you choose wisely, you will both enjoy the benefits of having your home-based business as well as add additional immediate value to your life. For instance, if you love to travel and you get involved with a travel business, your vacations just became legal expense deductions. Perhaps you love scotch and you create a scotch review blog with the intention to build a following and create revenue from the blog—you just created a legal entity that allows you to write off all the scotch you sample to write about on your blog.

How To Set Up Your Business

Setting up your business can be the most fun part of the process, mainly because it will not be much work on your part, yet you get a thrill when you create something new. The feeling never gets old for those who possess an entrepreneurial spirit. It can be as simple as enrolling in an already existing company that has an effective sales process for promoting its products. To do this, you find a cause and/or a product you believe in and a sponsor who is willing to support you in the process while you are not able to be fully active in the company. You simply sign up for the company; a multi-level marketing company often makes this simple. Beware, however, of anyone who promises to build your business for you; the business model is not designed to work this way and promises to do so could be a red flag—someone wants nothing more than to leverage your name.

Another option is to choose an area where you are confident you can make a difference in your community, such as mentor young athletes who aspire to go pro or teach a group of peers how to handle the emotional roller coaster high/low pressure of their professional careers. To engage in something of this nature, you need to consider something you are passionate about and where you are highly competent.

You can consult an attorney to decide how you form the business. As I write this, I have chosen an LLC as the structure for my company, which is sufficient for my business needs at this time. Simultaneously, we have a not for profit leg of our business that operates separately. A business can also be incorporated or be a sole proprietorship. I would recommend separating your business from your personal name and affairs. In most states it is as simple as applying for a business name and choosing your type (LLC, Inc., etc.), for a small fee (around $125), and once you have a name you apply at the IRS website for an EIN. Applying for the EIN should have no cost associated, so don't go through a site that asks you to pay a fee.

Once you have established an official business, you simply hire a bookkeeper to keep track of the spending you do for that particular business and any income that comes in as a result. Your tax strategist will be able to help show you the details of how the business affects your taxes. In the next segment you will review some of the potential savings you can take advantage of by having a home-based business.

you want to have more than one stream of income? Is what you have now not already helping you? The ideas behind multiple streams of income are based on a couple of things:

First of all, having multiple streams of income means that you have several sources of income that lead to your overall cash flow. That means you can have more income; it also means you're reducing the risk that your income could go away. The reduction of risk is huge. A lot of people talk about diversifying a portfolio and you've probably even heard the phrase, Don't put all your eggs in one basket; however, when it comes to income, very few people remember that diversification is key. Having multiple sources not only brings you more money, but it also allows you to have peace of mind knowing that you have the possibility of continued revenue should one or more of them unexpectedly disappear.

Let's focus now on the different types of income that you *could* have. As an athlete, you probably already have a few, or at are least looking to secure them:

- For instance, as a player, you get paid for the games that you play.
- There is also potential for a number of different endorsements to make extra money just being a spokesperson for a product, or for a company, or a brand.
- You might find yourself coaching or teaching other people to do some of the things that you've been able to do.

You may not wish to have too many active streams of income while you're active as an athlete because, of course, you have to focus on the game, but you can at least continue to prepare for them. Build the relationships now and continue to create possibilities for other future streams of income.

During your contract, and before you actually retire from the game, you want to add some serious think time pondering what else you will be able to do to bring in additional income. One of the things you might do is build a business. You read in another section about the tax advantages of having a home-based business, but think now about how that business could actually bring you more income. What if you had another $500, $2,000, $10,000 a month or more flowing in as extra income from a business you created. The only limitation to the list of possibilities is in your imagination; think about all the different ways you can have additional income!

You might choose to build other income streams through investments. That means to take the money you have earned as a player and invest it in a venture that creates another income stream. In the investment section, you will learn about **two different kinds** of investments you can have:

1. Investments that produce additional assets, which then grow in value and make your total assets and your net worth grow.
2. Then there are investments that produce income, which means actually creating cash flow in your pocket right now.

Either one of these is good for your overall wealth; you really want to choose investments based on what your overall goal is. Of course, I recommend having both.

In my e-book, *The Money Makeover: How to Easily Get Out of Debt, Create Wealth, and Build Passive Income*, I explore several options for creating income, which can be passive, residual, and active as well as securing assets that grow in value. You can check it out on Amazon.

amzn.to/1PNilGf

The next thing you want to think about is how you can really reduce your overall risk by creating various streams of income. For instance, if you have some really powerful endorsement deals because your brand and your name really works for you, you might be making a good bit of money just in those deals. In fact, sometimes players even make more than they can make on the field just by their endorsements. This is great for extra income, but one key piece you may also want to consider is if something should happen that causes your sports revenue to cease.

Maybe it's time for you to retire, or you have an injury that requires some time off, something happens in your family, or whatever it might be. As a general rule, as long as you continue to fulfill the terms of your contract, the endorsement deals don't necessarily go away. Usually you have signed contracts and while you may temporarily not be able to get out there on the field and pound away at your body because of some physical ailment, you should be able to keep your endorsements. Effectively, your endorsements reduce the risk of not having income during a season.

Other ways to reduce risk might be necessary when you do retire… assuming that you have strategically planned for investments… in multiple areas, and continue earning income in different ways. If one fails another might do extraordinarily well. Proper diversification should be taken up with your financial strategist; make sure that they have you on a well-diversified plan.

Each additional stream of revenue helps create diversification and reduce the risk to you as an investor. Chances are, you will most likely find, not so very long after you've retired, you feel you need something more to do with your life. This is the cool part! Not everyone has the option to create a true diversification of income in various areas, which is where your choices can become exciting.

Think of all the amazing ways you can earn money! Among all that are possible, you are likely to find a few that actually work for you and you would actually want to build. So let's discuss the three types of income you could generate when you decide to build those additional streams of income

One is called active income, another passive, and the other residual.

Active income is from you actually doing the work and getting paid in exchange for your effort. People who work a regular 9-5 job or other hours for W-2 pay, earn active income. People who run a business, even if that business is thriving, who are required to be on the job and in the job in order to make money, earn an *active income*. For instance, a financial planner doesn't make a lot of money if they don't do any work. For example: someone in the chiropractic industry, who when not regularly seeing patients, is not making money. Active income then, is the earned revenue for which you have to be actively participating in a given area, in order for any pay to flow.

Now, there's a lot of misconception about the next two. Often they're used interchangeably, but the truth is they really are not the same. Passive and residual incomes are two different types of revenue generation. Let's talk first about passive revenue.

You might hear the words *passive income* all the time. It's all over in various marketing scripts, where you hear everyone saying, Create passive income, and then they show you a system you can use to do that. Well, the truth is, what they are trying to engage you in is not true passive income! True passive income means that you do absolutely nothing in the process of earning it. You don't have to get up and go check on anything, you don't have to go to work, you don't have to build anything, and you don't have to do anything for the income to be generated, it just works – without any activity on your part.

Sounds kind of impossible, right? In fact, passive income is not so common. The only true passive income is the investments you make and the income they return. Your investment could be in real estate, the stock markets or bonds. You may receive coupon payments, from investing in bonds... that's the nature of true passive income.

So in order to get passive income, you have to first already have money, and then instead of you doing additional work, your previously earned money does the work to create additional income. Remember the little soldier golden coins? They, too represent passive income. The investments you make today and the decisions you make now can lead you to earning passive income, which is something many people never get to see until much later in life. You have a unique opportunity to build this easily and build it now. Are you feeling like a rock star about now?

Residual income… now this is where the real fun begins. Residual income comes to you when you first put in the work—you've done your duty, you've created a business or a concept or an idea or built something and it has grown and it is successful. Now, you no longer have to be actively involved for the money to be made. A great example of this is the network marketing industry. Many people actively build a business; they build a solid team and eventually don't have to be present because the team keeps working and the team leader is the one who keeps making money. Don't get the residual income period confused with the building phase of a network marketing business, during which time a lot of work is required.

In the beginning phase, you must consider network marketing *active income*. You have to work hard; you have to dig in and be seriously committed to the outcome. Just because you've built a team doesn't mean your income has grown to the point of being *residual*. If you're in a business or a company where as soon as you stop working, your team fades away and it's gone and then your money goes away too, that's not yet residual. Residual means you've already built a key revenue-generating foundation. Your business has grown to a point where it only requires a little maintenance here and there. You probably have hired someone to take care of that part or you check in on occasion and you just enjoy the income from it. It keeps growing; the systems are in place. It's making money simply because you've put the effort in the beginning and developed the right systems to ensure that the business keeps making money.

A dear friend of mine actually has three residual-based businesses. They are nearly passive for him it seems because he doesn't have to do a lot, but every Friday he has board meetings with those three different businesses. He makes sure everything is running smoothly They communicate information to him about what's going on in the business, and he gets to be informed and engaged in the business without ever needing to actually work in the business. Businesses like that are where you're really going to gain high-potential residual revenue. The coolest part about this kind of income is you can do it again and again and again, and that's exactly what my friend has done.

First, he decided he would build a financial business. He became a broker himself; if he remained an agent only, he would be working actively like anyone else. But he built a structure... a system where he was the broker and hired agents to do the work. In fact, he built a system so successfully designed he now has practices in many different cities around the United States. All he has to do is check in on Fridays and, voilà, he has a residual business! It is growing; it is making him money and it's continually increasing the amount of income that it generates for him.

In the beginning, however, he had to put in a healthy amount of work! And he didn't try to grow all three of his now successful businesses at once. He focused: he built a financial practice... got it running on its own... hired the right people... surrounded himself with a powerful team and then... he slowly stepped out. Now all he needs is that hour on Friday to keep his business thriving.

Rinse and repeat is the operative; his second business was created in much the same manner. The second one is in home healthcare. He built a business... he got involved... he did what he needed to do to put the systems in place, after which he was able to step away, have those board meetings on Fridays, and leave the business to earning the income. And he did it again with yet another business! He also practices as an attorney, where his active presence keeps him working 4-5 days per week. He continues his practice because he loves this work and would be bored without it.

So you can imagine the true essence of multiple streams of income this guy has. Three *residual* revenue-based businesses and another generating additional *active* income. His revenue is representative of a systematic cycle of passive investments derived from all the money that he earns, and also includes silent partnerships in other companies. He has, of course, investments in the market and many other areas. These are the cool results possible—to know and understand money early in your life—rather than learning much later. When is *now* the right time—because you have the time, the energy, the stamina, and in your case, the money—to make these things happen?

Chapter 13

STRATEGY #3: INVESTING | GROW ME THE MONEY

WHEN ENTERING THE investment game, the choices available to you, and all the different nuances within each, can be quite overwhelming. Without proper planning and stellar advice, even the most experienced investor can become baffled in the ocean of investment choices.

This chapter is designed specifically to give you a starting point and help you know what you should be looking for when making investment decisions. It is in no way intended to be a complete review of all the possible investments, nor is it a stand-alone guide on investing. Be sure to seek proper advice that is specific to your needs when investing. I do want to convey, however, the pointers in this chapter can help demystify the process a little bit and allow you to be informed of what you are looking for when you do go out to seek counsel on where to put your money.

- What are the numbers? Fees can make or break a financial plan; know them.

Takes Advantage Of Tax Breaks

One of the most substantial areas of sabotage to your investment can be good ole Uncle Sam. If you are not aware of the tax laws, you are likely to get caught up in an investment that will charge you right out of the very lifestyle for which you've been planning! There are, however, many different ways to approach tax concerns when it comes to investments. Next, let's address the *three types* of money you can have when it comes to saving.

1. Free money
2. Tax free money
3. Tax deferred money

Free money is simply money given to you by someone else. This would be, for instance, an employer match. This often happens when someone works for a sound company that has an investment tool like a 401(k) and matches a portion of your savings with their own money. While the 401(k) program is not guaranteed among pro-athletes, some of the leagues do offer special pension options. In the next chapter, you will further explore some other options available to you and the impact they can make on your plan.

Next in the pecking order of best money is *tax-free money*. Tax-free money is money that you can earn for which you will not have to pay taxes. The most common example of this is a Roth IRA. But don't run out and try to buy a Roth too quickly. If you are reading this book there is a high likelihood you make way too much money for a Roth to even be on your radar right now. Then there is the fact that the Roth IRA has age restrictions and you pay penalties if you use it before a specified age.

The good news is, in the next chapter I am going to show you a way to get tax-free money without the age or income restrictions.

There are other types of tax-free money as well. A more conservative investment, such as a municipal bond, is a good way for some to earn a non-taxable return on your investment. These are like loans to cities that pay a decent return for the low level of risk you must accept and you get a tax break for doing so. These are usually very long term as well and can make a nice addition to a portfolio but would not likely make up a large portion of it, nor would they grow very quickly.

Finally, you can look for tax-deferred money as a next best way to take advantage of tax breaks. While tax-deferred is better than no tax benefit, keep in mind that tax- deferred just means you are not *paying the tax until later*. Later, when it is time to pay, you hope taxes are as low or lower than now or that you have less income than you had when you were paying this tax.

For most people, tax-deferred money is not ideal as they are likely to make more money later in life and the high likelihood of a tax increase can be seen by even the most amateur onlooker as government debt continues to rise. However, for a short-term period, tax-deferred for a pro-athlete could allow a benefit that can reduce overall taxes.

In the next chapter you will read about paying taxes on the seed versus the harvest. For now, let's look at how a tax-deferred situation in the short-run may help. Let's say you choose a tax-deferred program that allows you to push the income forward and pay the tax at a later time. At the highlight of your career, this could be beneficial, as your income is likely at its highest and you are paying the top tax bracket on those extra dollars. After retiring, and you earn less for a while before your little soldiers catch up and pay you big revenues again, the tax-deferred pushed to this season could be beneficial. Collect on those moneys now when your tax bracket is lower.

quite frankly more exciting, is the idea of an **opportunity fund**. An opportunity fund is simply this:

> *Life throws many opportunities at us to take*
> *advantage of—great deals and moneymaking*
> *opportunities… if we are prepared to take action.*

◇◇◇◇◇◇◇◇◇◇◇◇◇

Most commonly, having cash on hand is the one thing that makes it possible to take advantage of these opportunities. If you have to wait until you get the funds together, you often miss the opportunity. While I have shared with you, and continue to share the importance of being cautious with anything that is today only, I want to stress here the power to have the ability to take action once you have realized an opportunity is, in fact, a good deal. Having an opportunity fund can help ensure you are positioned to take advantage of these opportunities when they show up.

So how does this fit in the flexibility section? Having key investments that afford you flexibility to access your cash within a short amount of time, like 24-48 hours, gives you the necessary cash power should an opportunity arise. It also helps you take the necessary 24-48 hours to fully analyze the opportunity to be sure it is the right move for you.

Does My Investment Fit My Life?

One thing many people forget to address when planning for investments is called the **suitability factor**. Does the investment I am choosing fit into my life and add value to me overall? There are some key aspects to consider here. For instance, an investment may have great returns and allow you all of the other features you want, but if the funds are being used to support a cause you do not believe in, it may not be the right fit for you.

Similarly, an investment may have all the benefits of meeting your desired cause, but if the numbers do not add up, it may be a huge mistake that can damage your overall portfolio. While it is a wonderful thing to support a cause you believe in, if the risk and reward factors do not line up, it is not an appropriate investment. You can choose to give to a particular cause and consider it part of your philanthropic interests, but I caution against considering it an investment or relying on it to yield returns.

When considering suitability, you want to pay attention to how an investment fits the following *seven areas*:

1. Does it meet the return requirements you need to stay on target with your goals?
2. Are the risks involved appropriate for the returns you will receive? And are the risks within your range of risk-taking acceptability?
3. Does the investment meet your values and allow you to sleep at night?
4. Does the investment have the likelihood to take you to your goals? Can you measure with some sense of certainty that the mix of investments you have chosen will allow you to reach them?
5. Does this investment fit within the overall portfolio and add value as a diversified part of the whole?
6. Does the investment portfolio you are putting together meet your needs for flexibility and access to cash?
7. Does the investment allow you the opportunity to leverage your funds for maximum returns for minimum risk?

As you build your portfolio with your financial strategist, you will likely be asked a series of questions about your lifestyle goals, the desires you have for giving, family, and other areas of your life. Be sure to fully consider each to the best you can foresee at this time. The more accurate you are in what you want, the more specifically you can design a portfolio together that will support your ultimate goal. And my number one rule:

Always plan for more than what you want. You never know when you might get a sudden new, and expensive, hobby!

◇◇◇◇◇◇◇◇◇◇◇◇◇

Who Should Help Me?

As you begin investing, it can be overwhelming to think about who should help you in the process. In fact, this is an area where most people begin to feel more than a little freaked out and nervous. This is perfectly normal; after all, the person or team you choose right now helps you make or break your financial future. Therefore, there are a few simple, but key areas, to keep in mind when choosing your financial strategy team. Keeping these in mind, you are on track to reach your goals and can feel secure and confident along the way.

First, does the strategy team you have selected have what it takes to help you reach your goals? Take the time to ask the following important questions:

- Do they have a good track record of helping their clients reach their goals?
- Do they have experience and the ability to create the desired outcome for you?
- Have they explored many strategies and selected those that they have found most supportive of their client goals or do they have only one go-to strategy they use for all clients?

It may be important to know that your team has the **ability and willingness** to guide you to the right mix for you, not just **what** they know.

Second, what does your financial strategy team have to gain by the decisions you make and where they guide you. Your team will certainly be paid in some way, either through a fee you pay for their guidance, through commissions, or both. This is why they are in business to help you and fees of some kind should be expected. Just be sure they are up front with you about how they get paid and what they have to gain using one investment over another.

A good fiduciary of your funds will be one whose interest is first and foremost in getting you to the right investments. In terms of being a financial advisor, if done right, they are naturally paid by what they do. What you need to know about is their philosophy. For instance, in my organization, we have a strong belief that by serving our clients to the highest and best good for their futures, we have more and better referrals and we ultimately win, even if the commissions or overall pay per client is reduced by choosing the strategies that best fit them rather than what pays us best. Does your financial team focus on your short term and long term success knowing they benefit most when you do?

Another issue about which you want to be aware when choosing your strategy team is how flexible your planners are to listen to your needs and desires and hear out the ideas you have, while also remaining firm in their suggestions for you if what you may think is good is really not in your best interest. While you want to be heard, and you may sometimes come into opportunities that are a perfect addition to your investment mix, you want a team that will let you know if you are off course with your planned ideas and be **bold enough to tell you it will not work**.

Ultimately, it is your portfolio and you get the final say, but would you really want a team that was afraid to tell you if you are messing up so at least you know and have the opportunity to make another, better choice? Likewise, you want a team that will give an honest look at what you are bringing in front of them to give you an analysis of the pros and cons to help you make the best final decisions. Because as a financial planner they may not benefit from a move you make with your money… this should never be a reason for them to ignore or dismiss the idea without a fair look. Be sure they are on *your* team first.

The underlying purpose is to support you, and that is what their actions should reflect. It is ok to fire your financial team if you feel they are not working for your best good. However, think twice before you fire your strategist simply because they disagree with you—it is actually their job—if what you are suggesting does not propel you toward your goals. Just like a coach, they tell you what you should do and what will work best. In the end, however, it remains your choice and responsibility to execute that guidance.

Chapter 14

STRATEGY #4: CREATING A SAFETY NET THAT PAYS

WHEN PLANNING FOR your financial future, it may seem like insurance is the last thing you need to worry about. Even though it may be one of the farthest things from your mind as a young, energetic, healthy being, it is actually the best and most important time for you to think about it. There are many types of insurance you may consider… for the purposes of learning, focus on the two major types you need to consider: life and disability.

You already carry protection against the loss of your car, and maybe even many of your bigger assets, like a house, a boat, RV, etc. We are trained as a society to protect our stuff, but what about the income you require in order to buy and maintain having all these fun things? *Disability insurance* is, for many people, one of the most overlooked, underused, and missing pieces of the financial puzzle. Disability insurance could easily be called income protection. It is the assurance that if something goes wrong and you can no longer work, you are covered and able to get paid during the period where you cannot work. There are two types: short term and long term.

If you have signed a contract as an athlete, you likely have some sort of *short-term disability insurance* built in. That is, if you sign a contract and become injured, you are likely to get paid even while injured—until your contract is fulfilled. This depends on your contract agreement, of course, so be sure to really know what your contract says. But, what are your plans for the time following the end of your contract? The following questions are critical for making decisions:

- If you are injured during a contract period, but still cannot play after that term is over, how do you get paid?
- Who will sign a new contract with an injured player?
- How can you protect yourself?

This is where *long-term disability insurance* comes into play; it is a way you can protect against the loss of income that would occur if you could no longer play.

Insurance regulations control how much you can actually cover, but on a regular policy you can cover up to 60% of your regular income. Playing it right and paying for the coverage with after-tax dollars, you could bring home very close to what you had while working in the event an injury would occur.

For athletes already in the league, there are many variances to how a disability policy may work. The structure of your disability policy is based on the original contract (i.e. your actual current income) as well as potential future earnings based on your potential. Obviously, the shorter average play life for a football player would be less than that of a baseball player, so the structure of the disability and what is covered would vary accordingly. The purpose of the policy is to protect your ability to earn.

The sport, your position played, what is covered (i.e. total loss or specific body parts such as an arm for a pitcher), your total potential future earnings, and where you are in your career... are all factors affecting your eligibility and cost for coverage.

Consult with someone who specializes in disability coverage to make sure you select what is best and most cost effective for you. Your financial strategist likely has relationships with agents they have vetted to be sure you get not only the best deal, but the plan most appropriate for you. As you can see, this is an area you want to think about now... while you are healthy, the coverage is relatively inexpensive, and you can actually gain access to it.

Another critical area many do not want to think about while young and healthy is life insurance. You are young and probably feel like you are going to live forever. I can't say I blame you. I feel that way too. But I have learned a few tricks with life insurance that are going to change the way you look at it. As you begin to discuss this critical element, you will explore three things you want to think about as you make your insurance decisions. Also, you will look at a bonus of using life insurance products that have protected many famous and wealthy individuals from having their wealth stripped away with the unexpected occurrence of lawsuits, settlements, bankruptcies, and even nasty divorces. Before you make any decisions, you need to know the answer to the following questions:

- What is your purpose for the insurance?
- How much do you really need and for how long?
- What is the most effective way to reach your goals?
- Bonus: How can you legally protect your income from parasites?

First, ask yourself why you would want life insurance. Its primary purpose is to protect those you have left behind. This can be your family, your extended family and friends, or others you care about. Typically, the coverage is used for those who have responsibilities within their families and want to be sure that if something happens to them, their families will be taken care of. Some, though, use life insurance as a way to be sure their dream of building a legacy, supporting a cause, and building a foundation is met even if they do not get to live to make it happen with their earnings.

Whatever your reason, know the primary focus of insurance is on what you leave behind. There are some creative strategies, however, which use life insurance as a loophole to plan a retirement where you do not have to pay taxes on your income. You will read more about that later in this chapter.

Knowing your underlying purpose for using insurance helps you to answer the next important question. How much do you need? For instance, if you goal is to make sure your family can maintain a lifestyle you have created for them, then the amount you need is based on the income you would have been earning… assuming you lived. If you want to start a foundation, you could base the amount of life insurance on the funds that are needed to get it started.

For many people, the basic rule of coverage to protect your family is equal to 10 times the annual income you currently earn in life insurance coverage. This is an ambitious amount and may be a little excessive for most. I like to focus more on what you actually need in order to maintain the lifestyle of those you love. For instance, if you are no longer here to need your Rolex or flashy car, these expenses do not need to be planned for. I suggest sitting down with a planner who is more focused on you than on how much insurance they can write for you. Having enough is important, but having too much can get expensive and tap into the funds you could be enjoying if you opt for plan A—which of course is to live!

Another important area of insurance planning is the consideration of how long you need the coverage. The idea of life insurance is to cover you until you have lived long enough to make the money and meet your goals with your income. Many advisors who have made a name for themselves in the financial industry will tell you to buy term and invest the difference. While this could be true if properly structured investments were truly purchased with the savings, in most circumstances this does not prove true. My philosophy is more about buy the type of insurance that best meets your needs and find it at the cheapest rate possible from a credible and asset strong company. For most of the clients I have worked with, term life insurance just does not hit the mark to meet their overall needs.

That leads us to the next piece. What is needed to actually reach your goals? If all you want is to protect yourself during your earning years and nothing after, you could buy term. However, for most you want a longevity plan, and one that gives back as you continue to live longer rather than checking out early. Life insurance proceeds is not a check you want your family to cash any time soon. But, what if there was a way that as you are planning for that dreaded day you could simultaneously build up some of the assets you need to support your retirement goals? Using the right products and structure with your life insurance has the potential to be one of the best parts of your investment portfolio.

So I have teased you with hints enough; it is now time to start sharing a little about how you can actually use insurance products to create a more powerful portfolio and even receive tax-free income!

Let's lay the foundation first of why you would want a tax-free income.

The first thing you need to understand is the
IRS can be on your side if you just know the rules.

◇◇◇◇◇◇◇◇◇◇◇◇◇

While many are not so fond of Uncle Sam, those who take the time and make the investment to hire the best planners can actually use the tax laws to their benefit. It is time you get those benefits, too.

Note: I am going to keep this simple so it is easy to digest. Don't let this simplification be a trigger for you to try to do all this planning on your own. These are advanced tips, and knowing them can arm you with what you need—to be sure the financial strategist you choose takes advantage of these strategies for you.

First, there are two major ways of saving according to the IRS. One is called qualified dollars and the other unqualified. While it may sound like one is better since it is qualified, the term just means is this has met the IRS rules to be tax deferred. Tax deferred simply means you don't have to pay the taxes on the income until later, when you use the money for retirement. Sounds like a deal, doesn't it? In fact, most retirement specialists have used this option for years, especially since the creation of the 401(k) in 1978 and its inception in 1980. You have probably heard of the 401(k) and even the IRA. These and other accounts are commonly referred to as an ERISA classification for the Employee Retirement Income Security Act. These are retirement accounts, which give your funds a special treatment, where any money put in them can be deducted from your income for the current year and you delay paying taxes on it until later.

Put simply, these funds are designed to get you to not touch your money and make sure you have money for your retirement. While there are some great benefits in these accounts, the trade-off is not worth it for most people. You will see some benefits and drawbacks in a comparison in the next section.

So why do so many people use these types of retirement accounts? Let me explain by telling the story of the ham.

A very curious little girl wanted to know why her mom always cut off the ends of the ham to bake it in the oven. Her mom replied, I don't know. That's the way my mother did it. So the mom, now as curious as the daughter asked her own mother who replied, I don't know. It's just how my mother did it. Finally, with the curiosity getting the best of all of them they asked the great grandmother who said, It was because when I was young and poor, and I got the meat, I found my oven was too small!

The moral of the story... sometimes the way you do certain things now is because it is all you know from how you've been taught; yet it may not be the only way, nor the best way to do it now. When it started, it may have been the best option; now, it is no longer true. This is how I view the 401(k) and IRA plans.

When the products were first made available, people needed a way to save for retirement that was easy and made it more affordable for them. If they could defer taxes, then the actual immediate cost to them was less. Remember, we were moving from a time when pensions were normal and we didn't have to save our own money in a more self-directed plan where it was up to us to save for our future. This tax deferred benefit made it possible for far more people to afford to save.

Top that off with the fact that employers, ever so eager to no longer have to save for your pension plan payments, could also save money in their tax bill if the money was deducted from your taxable income. Employers have to match, for instance, our social security tax paid. If you reduce your taxable income, employers reduce their taxable wages. So, companies began offering employer matches to incentivize employees to participate in the 401(k) programs. This was great. Free money. When the opportunity was first implemented, the matches were much better than they tend to be today so it made sense to take advantage of them.

As mentioned previously, I always advise my clients to take money in this order:

- *Free money*—money given to you by someone else, like an employer as a reward for something, without requiring you to work for it. Some leagues have pension plans that offer free money. See the discussion of pensions later in this section.
- *Tax-free money*—money you can earn and save without paying taxes on it as it grows. This is what you read about earlier as paying tax on the seed, or beginning amounts put in, and not needing to pay tax on the harvest, or the growth of your money.
- *Tax deferred money*—money you can use without paying taxes on it until a later date when you actually use it. This would be to avoid paying tax on the seed, but paying tax on the entire harvest.
- *Taxable money*—money you just have to pay taxes on no matter what you do, such as your net income from this year. (Reference the home based business section to review how to reduce the taxable portion of your income.) This is like paying tax on the seed when you plant it and paying tax on all the growth that accumulates from it as well.

Unfortunately, free money often comes with a price. You are not allowed to touch your 401(k) or IRA money until at least the currently designated age of 59.5 or you pay a penalty—in addition to paying taxes on the money that is counted against your ordinary income. What's worse, the IRS is now going to tax you on the *entire amount*, both what you saved in the beginning and all its growth over the years you saved it.

Is this really a good deal for you, the taxpayer who saved paying taxes on a dollar (around $.35), or the IRS who gets paid for taxes on the full eight dollars it turned into before you could use it (around 2.80)? Assume you saved $100,00—that grows to $800,000—in this tax deferred way and saved $35,000 in taxes. You now get to pay the IRS $280,000 ($800,000*35%) for the privilege of saving that $35,000. The difference, however, is an extra $245,000 paid to Uncle Sam, reducing your account value to $520,000 after taxes.

Uncle Sam sure had one smart Aunt Sally when he created these tax laws!

◇◇◇◇◇◇◇◇◇◇◇◇◇

If your employer provides the free money, this changes the story a little. Let's say they offered a 100% match so you now saved $200,000 that has grown to $1,600,000. After you pay the IRS its 35% ($560,000), you still have $1,040,000 remaining. That makes the 401(k) suddenly more attractive. But this is not so common anymore, and as a pro-athlete, you need to check with your league to see if you even have a 401(k) program. You may find some opportunities like this in your post athlete career as well, so this is worth you knowing the possibilities… just in case.

Now, here is the good news regarding free money. Some leagues do have pension plans that match the dollars you put away. For instance, the NFL has a pension that puts away a 2:1 match[3], which means for every $1 you save, the NFL puts away $2 on your behalf. If you become eligible, that is play for two or more years you are vested. Vested simply means you get access to the money put away for you. If you should leave the league before becoming pension eligible, what you saved still belongs to you; you just wouldn't get the matching part. Funds for this account are eligible for withdrawal starting at age 45. Additionally, the NFL offers an annuity program that can begin withdrawals at age 35, but requires at least 4 years eligible playtime.

The NBA offers a very generous pension plan as well. Within only three years participation, an NBA athlete is eligible for a pension plan ranging from $56,988 to $195,000 with 11 years or more played

---

3   http://www.delducasports.com/assets/files/Summary-of-NFL-Player-Benefits.pdf

(Riddix, 2010)[4]. Additionally, the NBA 401(k) plan offers a 1.4 to 1 match for dollars saved.

The MLB offers a very flexible plan, with only 43 days required before becoming pension eligible, and fully vests the retirement fund after 10 years. The NHL focuses on the number of games of eligibility, requiring 160 games.

It is fairly obvious here you should consult your financial advisor for what has changed more recently and discover how your specific industry approaches pensions. The bottom line is, you must be on top of your financial future or it will feel like it is suddenly on top of you when it comes time for you to retire.

The IRA works the same as the 401(k) for our purposes here, except there is not going to be any free money from your employer to help offset the additional taxes. Remember, we have simplified the messages here to make it understandable without overwhelming you in areas it is not your job to know. We do hold seminars to teach this more in depth for those who want to know more.

Consider this as a Playbook that is designed to be sure you know what goes on with your money and is not intended to be a substitute to reach out and find a financial strategist to work with you in your specific situation.

Let's move on to insurance products and how they can support you in reaching your goals, and explore once again the primary purpose for insurance. Insurance is meant to be a protection from a loss. In most cases, you use various insurance products as a protection against the loss due to injury, death, and even to protect our assets. But what about using them to cover losses due to future tax increases, and better yet, losses of income to just pay taxes at current rates?

---

4   http://www.investopedia.com/financial-edge/0710/top-pro-athlete-pension-plans.aspx

As you may have guessed, you have stepped into the ranks of the wealthy and the knowledge to which they have had access for a long time. The truth is, you don't have to be wealthy to take advantage of what I am about to teach you, but if you want to retain that status, it would benefit you to pay attention here. You may even want your family members and friends to read this section so they can also use these strategies and create a better future for themselves.

You have already looked at how paying taxes on money later can really dip into your funds, and the truth is we were being kind assuming the IRS is only going to hit 35% of your money. The higher your income, the more they will take off the top. Also, do you really think taxes are likely to go down or even remain the same by the time you retire? With our current national deficit how else will that be managed other than with our own future earnings?

With that in mind, let me show you one of the simplest and most cost effective ways you have available *right now* to avoid paying those higher tax rates. Starting today, you can easily set yourself up for success by using insurance products with cash value accumulation (this means your money grows inside the insurance policy) to grow your income. Then, because the IRS regulations allow you to borrow money from yourself from the accumulated cash in the policy, you can later take out money to use for your retirement income as a loan to yourself rather than as income and use it completely tax-free! Add to this structure the use of what we call an indexed fund for your cash value in the policy and you get to take advantage of the growth in the market without taking on the risks that are typically part of investing in the market.

How can this be done you ask? It's simple: the insurance companies work with fund balances way bigger than any single investor and can build a portfolio that can take some of the negative hits, while still gaining as a whole. What better way to have the best and brightest

I know you are most likely to live almost forever, doesn't it feel good to know that if for some unforeseen reason you do not, your family is taken care of?

Now for one of my favorite benefits of using life insurance products for a person in your position… someone with some influence and a lot of money, which others are likely to target. Funds held in life insurance products are established to provide protection from the perils of bankruptcy, lawsuits, and divorce. Remember O.J. Simpson? He got into plenty of trouble and yet his income just keeps coming in. How did he do that? His annuity products were set up prior to getting in trouble in a manner to fully protect them from lawsuits, court fines, and all attacks on him financially, so as to not penetrate his annuity funds.

While I hope you are not planning on getting into that kind of trouble, it would be nice to know you are protected should something crazy ever happen, wouldn't it? I bet Tiger Woods never thought he would get caught or his wife would lose it on him.

Who knows what the future holds? You hope life is a smooth ride, but plan for it to be bumpy!

◇◇◇◇◇◇◇◇◇◇◇◇◇

And finally, one of my favorite reasons to use life insurance as a framework for investments—Leverage! When properly structured, a cash value building life insurance policy can provide a type of banking system where you can access funds for other activities, such as investing in a business, real estate, or other opportunities. What you need is an ultra flexible repayment plan where you have a chance to have your funds invested twice.

How can this work? It is actually quite simple, though much is involved. For our purposes here, just know if you have a life insurance policy with cash value that is properly structured, you can borrow from that policy's cash value at a low rate and use the funds to invest in something that can generate a return while the cash value of your policy remains invested in the market index and earns a return. We call this double dipping, and in the money business, that is a good thing. If you want more information on how to use your policy as leverage, check out *The Tax Free Retirement* by Patrick Kelly. This is a strategy we often use for our athletes who want to save but also want to have easy access to their funds should a good investment opportunity arise. Ask your advisor or contact our office to see more about how this can be structured for you.

Earlier I promised you a review of the benefits and drawbacks of the retirement plans you discussed. Here you go.

Retirement Planning Advantages and Disadvantages[5]

Benefits of 401(k) and other ERISA plans
- Potential employer match adds value to your total
- Tax deferred income savings can be saved as well, increasing total savings
- Protected from bankruptcy judgments

Drawbacks of 401(k) and other ERISA plans
- Full earnings growth is taxed as withdrawn
- Not fully protected in divorce
- Not fully protected against IRS tax debts
- Not protected against criminal activity
- Cannot access funds before 59.5 without penalty
- Fees can potentially be high

---

5   http://www.nolo.com/legal-encyclopedia/can-judgment-creditors-go-after-my-retirement-accounts.html

Benefits of Life Insurance Plans

- Fully protected from bankruptcy
- Potentially protected from divorce
- Fees can be smaller than mutual funds and other plan fees
- Protected from law suits and civil judgments
- Can provide fully tax-free income
- Provides liquidity of funds as needed
- Offers a leveraged portfolio solution

Drawbacks of Life Insurance Plans

- Requires purchase of life insurance for a fee and requires eligibility
- Does not typically offer extremely high rates of return
- Can be taxable if you cancel the policy

So what are the types of life insurance products I use? There are many options, and like any good advisor, I always choose those which, after careful analysis, best fit my clients' specific needs. However, some of my favorites, which seem to fit in the portfolio plan for most people, are Indexed Universal Life policies and certain Indexed Annuities. Why? At the time of writing this book, some of the best benefits I know came from these investment products, and because the market is competitive, all the top insurance companies keep competing to come out with continually better products that are both more powerful investment tools and cheaper to the client. That is what I call a win for everyone.

Chapter 15

STRATEGY # 5: GET INVOLVED IN A CAUSE

ONE OF THE not often thought of areas of financing and understanding money is actually more about the giving piece. Giving, doesn't that take away from you, you ask? The truth remains: people who are givers by nature typically have the best financial resources and the best financial picture of anyone else. Why? Because they're accustomed to having a big why… a cause behind what they're doing. So, in this section you're going to read about getting involved in a cause and using that to fuel your financial future. This doesn't mean you get involved for the sole purpose of gaining from a particular cause; it simply means it gives you a reason significant enough keep moving forward in something meaningful you can add to the world, which keeps you on track—even with your own financial goals.

The first thing you have to do to get involved with a cause is focus on something you care about. What is it about how the world works for which you have some concern or passion? What happens and why do you care about making a change for something good in that particular element of life? Many people find that their real cause, the one that really moves them the most, often has something to do with their own situation. Spend some time considering the following questions:

- What exactly was your upbringing?
- What were your experiences?
- What are some areas where you wished someone could have helped you in your life?
- How did someone did help you in your life?

These are great ways to identify and connect with a cause that can move you and keep you on track with your own goals.

Think about your life. Go through the events of your life from the time you can remember—up through now. What are some things that have shown up for and you found yourself saying:

- I'm going to change that.
- Somebody should change that?
- What can I do to help?
- I wish I could make a difference.

When you find those areas in your life, you will recognize the places where you can now make a difference. And again, supporting this cause can lead you to something, which can set you up more specifically in your own life, because there's a passion and a reason behind it.

Keep in mind your choices don't always have to be charitable causes; it could be a cause that has something more to do with your own family, the people around you, or your own city. It doesn't have to be a broad scale cause; it can be small or large. It doesn't have to be something you start on your own. In fact, I don't recommend starting your own foundation or starting your own process while you're still involved in the game.

Focus on your game; give to a cause.

Giving doesn't always mean money! It can mean time, as well. Keep in mind that the biggest resource many places need are people who are willing to give their time. Give financially; give knowing it always comes back to you, but more importantly… show up and give of your time.

Can you imagine the excitement if you worked with a group of children, for instance and as a pro-athlete you gave of your time… to read a book at a library or to play with them at the playground? They'll have those memories for the rest of their lives and the pictures you have taken with them will be shown to their kids for decades. And then one day they're going to show their grandchildren and say When I was seven… or whatever their age was at the time. They're going to use your name in their story of a pro-athlete who took the time to play with them and had such a wonderful time. He is my hero, is the message they will share.

Know that whatever cause you're going to get involved in, your presence as well as your money can make a big difference Just be wise in choosing something that you actually do care about, as will be revealed when you respond to the following:

- What knocks on your door?
- What keeps you awake at night?
- If you do watch the news, what is it you see that disgusts you the most?
- What warms your heart the most when you see something good happen?

From this perspective, you are better prepared to let your cause drive your life. In many cases you can't do for yourself what you can do for others. I don't know the human dynamics behind this, but I remember having met so many people in my lifetime who, for whatever reason, carry a heavy burden on their backs... a tremendous financial struggle to reach their financial goals if they perceive the purpose has anything to do with them.

For one, your *future-self* is just that... a *future-self*. It's a myth, right? You really don't exist yet. Feeling rather nebulous... out there waiting for you to reach one day, but in many cases it's just not real enough for most people to put something toward a *future-self* they can't really emotionally or mentally connect to just yet. Hopefully, if you've gone through some of my seminars you're grown fully able to connect to your *future-self through imagination*, but in general, many people struggle with the very concept. You are encouraged to use our lifestyle planners on the www.financialdevelopment.orgsite to connect to your *future-self* concerning the lifestyle you want for him or her.

Since most struggle to connect with a *future-self,* let this cause you have chosen be your why. If you're not willing to save and to create a spending plan that gets you to your financial goals, focus on the cause, the thing that drives you, keeps you up at night, or provides you the courage to push one more set when you think you've maxed out. What is it that drives you and keeps you going, thinking, and pressing on when times are tough? Whatever that cause is, it's what got you here. Now, you just need a cause with just as much passion and just as much drive to keep you going financially. Imagine the difference you could make in that cause if you are, say, true to your financial goals. Let that cause drive your why, the cause that you come to realize and understand when you respond to the following questions:

- Why would I want to help?
- Why would I do this?
- Why would I save and be willing to pass on buying that Bugatti today knowing that I can make that difference now and in the future?

Let your why continue to drive you! The why that comes from your heart can literally be the fuel that helps you push right through and reach all of your financial goals.

Another piece of where getting involved in a cause can actually help you—creating relationships with those who administer the cause. You want to get involved with them and let them know who you are. Let them know you want to help...ask them, How can I help? What do you need? You're going to create relationships when they see you want to give, help, and offer support. Creating relationships is a huge part of what drives us and keeps us on target. Once you develop strong, sincere relationships, it's just natural to want to make them happy. We really don't have to ask whether you want to make them feel good—a sense of accountability is suddenly there that you said you were going to do something so now you have to do it!

Use these relationships to keep you on track. Make a promise... you might even go as far to make a huge financial promise to a cause that you plan to give to 10 to 20 years from now, through a promise to the relationship you've created with those running the foundation. You now have a reason to stay on target so that you can keep that promise!

I'm not saying that everything that you do should be driven by your own needs to reach your financial goals. I'm simply saying that in many cases you're willing to do more and work harder for other people than you are for yourself, and if that's the case for you a cause about which you are passionate could literally be the driving force that allows you to have everything you've ever wanted. That cause can be as simple as taking care of your own family or as bold as feeding all the hungry people of the world.

I love this quote by Zig Ziglar, If you want to get what you want, help enough people get what they want. And there are many reasons that philosophy works. It works because when you help other people get what they want you automatically set up a reciprocation system, where something is done for you, you feel need to give to another. In addition, it works because when you do for others there's a different drive that comes into play. And regardless of your spiritual beliefs, there is a certain law governing the Universe that says Givers get. You don't have to be religious for this law to apply. If you are religious, it applies to you the same as to those who aren't. It is as clear and definite as the law of gravity.

My former father-in-law started a program called *Living with a Cause*. The whole premise of this organization and his purpose behind it was because he recognized the value other people place on doing something for someone else as opposed to himself or herself. And literally, he got an entire congregation of people to commit to this cause and now he's spread it across the city and it's starting to spread across the state and globe.

The idea behind supporting causes actually lies in the sacrifices people are willing to make for the benefit of others. For example, how hard would it be for you to give up having a soda? It can be downright close to impossible to think about giving up something you love, but to say, Hey, I'm not going to drink soda for 30 days and every penny I would have spent on it I'm going to donate to some worthy cause that I believe in, for some reason really gets people moving.

In fact, one of my friends in that church several years ago was very heavy and loved to eat fast food frequently; he made a decision. He had tried to diet... he had tried to do everything he could just to get in shape, but at the end of the day instant gratification drove him and he would give in and eat the fast food. After implementing the *Living with a Cause* system in this area of this life, he gave up fast food, and every time he wanted to eat fast food he donated the amount he would have spent on it to a bucket he had set up. At the end of each month he collected all the funds he had not spent on fast food; it was wintertime, and he used the money to buy gloves for a shelter that had young children.

These were children who didn't have much and it was cold and we were having a snowy winter in Ohio. They wanted to play in the snow but they just didn't have any gloves. This was a cause that meant something to my friend. The best part about it, he didn't think about the fast food or what he was giving up, and every time he passed on the fast food he thought, T*hat's one more child that can be playing warmly in the snow if I just let go!* The children's needs drove him and he saved. He saved and he saved. The most beautiful part of this entire story is not only did he have money for over 100 pair of gloves over the course of his cause, he also lost a ton of weight, was healthier and more in shape, and felt better than he had in all his life.

That is what using a cause to drive you can do for you. Yes, it's about the cause, but the truth is, at the end of the day, it's almost impossible to be deeply involved in a cause and not gain something personally yourself. So let your cause drive your why—create those relationships and the next thing you'll want to think about is to create a movement of your own using your influence. Now, again, I want to reiterate the time to build your own movement is not when you're actively involved in your sport; it is obvious your focus and passion has to remain on your training, and the need to improve and create the win/win with your own contracts. Creating a movement at the wrong time might be costly to your career. If you have an idea for a movement you'd like to create, you have enough people who are onboard to do it, and you can just be the face of it… then yeah, go for it.

get after that first one can be a bonus, and you can use each new contract to grow your dreams to a bigger degree. Besides, with all the changes always occurring in the pro-athlete contract arena, it is difficult to know what contracts will be offered next year, let alone be fully confident of the actual path of your entire career. With that in mind, it is best to look at some of the risks you face as an athlete, such as:

- Risk of injury
- Risk of non-performance
- Risk of Off the field or Off the court issues

The first risk is probably obvious to you. The risk of injury is huge. You play in a sport that requires you trade your physical body, stamina, and ability for pay. This works well as long as you maintain the expected level of physical ability. The best thing you can do to protect yourself in this area is to be smart while playing and when off the field. Avoid stupid moves that risk your physical being and keep yourself ready to play hard at all times. This includes avoiding distractions such as money worries that could take your focus off the game and get you hurt.

The second risk… well, it is all about you, the performer. You have to keep performing in order to keep the contracts coming. Sometimes, you may even find yourself with an extremely short, trial-period contract before you get the big one, which is quite common in the NFL. Stay focused on your game. This is the point where it may be worth the investment in a performance coach if you don't already have one. If you find yourself losing focus from some mind-game going on inside you as you go for it big, hire help. Don't wait and hope you can train enough, work out enough, or try hard enough to overcome the mind stuff. Get help early; stay focused on your performance. Knowing you have your money concerns handled can also help you stay focused. If you don't have to worry about how your life may fall apart should you not get that next contract, you can relax a little more than the guy beside you—and that little edge could be what keeps you ahead of the competition. There will always be someone bigger, faster, and stronger than you. Stay focused where it matters and your It Factor will keep you going and give you the edge to secure another contract.

Let's talk now about the third—and most prevalent—risk you may face to your career: the nasty triggers known as off the field or off the court offenses. Totally within your control, if I might put it politely, these are misjudgments on your part about what behavior is acceptable. But then… I guess I am not here to be polite; I am here to keep you paid for life, so let's be real with each other. These offenses are the *stupidity tax* you must pay when you make decisions that can cost you your livelihood. Your payment can range from fines paid from your earnings to the total loss of your contract… to the possibility of jail time.

You are young, and having access to all this cash at an early age has been the stimulus for some really stupid behavior athletes may not otherwise have opportunity or reason in which to engage. It may seem fun at the time, but I am telling you, don't do it! If you find yourself in a situation where you may be encouraged to make a decision you know is not good for your career, have a buddy system set up in advance. Make sure you partner with someone who is not likely to want to enjoy moments of temporary lapse of brain function with you. Have someone you can call or text to come get you out of the situation.

Where I grew up, you called that having someone who would knock some sense into you! A code word is always helpful. Even when drunk or high you might still be able to send a code word so your buddy can come get you out of a situation before you make a really stupid mistake. Set this up, now! I will understand when you call later to thank me. Oh, and if it should happen to save you thousands or even millions of dollars by saving your contract… well, then you can take my team and me to dinner as a thank you!

Exiting the Game

Regardless of how well you play it, the day will come when you know…
it's time for you to leave the game. Whether you get in a few good years
and then cash out and live a nice life like Magic Johnson or stick around
for years like Brett Favre or Shaquille O'Neil… at some point you will
be ready to retire and leave the rough play to the young kids you've by
then likely been mentoring.

We discussed in the beginning of *The Money Shot* some of the factors
to consider when exiting the game. Be sure to go back and review this
section if you want to re-examine some key points here. You may also
want to mark this section to revisit a little later in your career as well.

Understand that leaving the game is a natural part of the process.
But before you get to that point in your career, it is critical to schedule
an appointment with your financial strategist to be sure your financial
plan is on track to keep you going beyond your exit. For instance, you
should have set up an income plan for how you will get paid when you
leave the game. I reiterate, Now is the time to start looking at when your
post-game pay will begin, how the timing affects the total you can get
paid, and having the income structured to last for as long as you need
or want it to last.

The strategy to exit the game should start for your financial planner
at the moment you begin the relationship. Then, when you actually
near the exit date, make sure to start talking about this next phase of
your strategy with your planner six months or a year prior to leaving the
game. The more time you give your planner to set up your affairs, the
better. Ask your planner when you first create your tactics how much
time in advance you need to let them know. If you are getting at least an
annual review, and if you decide to retire during the next one, let your
financial team know— so they can review with you what it means for
you financially—to continue through another contract or commit to
retire. Communication is key to achieve your overall success.

Chapter 17

STRATEGY #7: SLEEP ON IT

Delay Big Decisions Overnight and Save Millions

WHEN YOU HAVE a lot of money, the first thing that often happens is suddenly having opportunities to purchase things you've always wanted and fulfill dreams you never imagined until now that could really come true. The opportunities just suddenly appear and you can purchase everything you ever wanted, with nothing to stop you. All of a sudden you find yourself on a buying frenzy... buying... buying... buying.

You see the same thing happen when people hit the lottery, which is similar to what you've done, except you did it through hard work and skill. All of a sudden, you find yourself in a status of wealth with more money than you could ever dream possible. If you never took the time to really get to know how to interact with money, or how to have money as we've discussed before, it can be overwhelming and you just

Sometimes might change your mind and say, You know what, this isn't right for me. And at other times you might instinctively make a decision and move forward. A side note here, don't worry about the deposit; in the grand scheme of things, if you put down $200, $500 even a $1000 deposit and you decide not to move forward, it's okay. Think instead about the thousands of dollars you just saved yourself not purchasing something that just wasn't right for you.

Let's get back to *what to do* in the 24-to-48 hour holding period. Before you get to that buy moment, have a process for making financial decisions. Understand up front how you know it's a yes! I often teach a class on how to make a decision and get clear on whether you have a yes or a not now purchase. The most common reviews of this course reflect techniques people have used over and over involve:

1. Take a breath and pause.
2. Ask, Am I making an emotional decision or is this a logical one?
3. How will I feel about **having** made this purchase in a day, a week, or a month?
4. How will I feel about **not having** made this purchase in a day, a week, or a month?

As you can see, there's a whole process here that actually walks you through how to determine the yes, or not now, question.

There are many times your gut may be the best judge of your next course of action. How do you know when to move quickly and when to take your time? Perhaps it is a business deal in which you would like to get involved. This is when it is critical to take that moment, breathe and follow a proven path. But after that, how do you make your decision wisely?

You first ask the emotion versus logical question, Does this make logical sense or am I caught up in the emotion of a great sales presentation where someone is showing me all the benefits and I really haven't had the chance to process both sides?

First, try the pause activity; give yourself a chance to step back and identify if you're acting based on emotion or logic.

Another thing you want to do is ask yourself, Does this fit my goals? Many times it may fit some kind of goal, right? You might have an immediate desire to drive a Bugatti but it doesn't fit the **real goals** of your *future* life. Is this particular experience really going to create so much joy in your life that it supersedes all the things you have to trade to get it? For instance, the beach house in the future? Again as a side note: Remember you can always rent the Bugatti, enjoy the driving experience and then let somebody else pay the rest of the bill. Not a bad idea—yes?

What is your system? Ask yourself. I can show you here how to go through a process but the truth is, it has to be a process that works for you and makes sense for you as you find clarity in the following:

- Is it going to bring me the most joy?
- Is this purchase part of my overall goals and what I really want?
- How long will I get to enjoy this result?
- How long will I need to take care of it and/or pay for it?
- How often will I be able to enjoy this?

A good analogy of this decision-making is finding you're in season in a cold climate a full nine months out of the year and that much-desired Bugatti sits in your home somewhere else in the warm climate and there are only three months out of the year you get to drive it. Even then you're training, busy with family, catching up with friends and find you get to drive it about 20 days out of a year. With all that being said, expensive price tags suddenly become a little less appealing, don't they? Answering this line of questions can help you get clear about how much value an item brings to your life—versus how much it costs.

Let's take this line of reasoning a bit further and look at when it's a business opportunity put in front of you, and the questions you might consider:

- When does this pay the returns?
- How guaranteed are these returns?
- Am I likely to stick in this investment for the long term?
- How long do I have to keep my money tied up in this?
- Who is guaranteeing that it's going to work?
- What are the risks involved now?
- Can I afford to risk the money that I'm putting out for this business opportunity if it doesn't work?
- Will this create any awkward situations in friendships that I have if this doesn't work?
- How will I manage and navigate all of the moving pieces?

These are all questions you want to ask before you say yes and sign on any dotted line! Again, what is the system and the process that works best for you?

There are sample worksheets on our site www.financialdevelopment. org, which you can use if you haven't developed your own decision-making process. What I encourage you to do, though, is to take these worksheets, scratch the questions that don't resonate with you and add to it the questions that do matter to you. Create your own worksheet; one you will willingly use every time you have a big financial decision looming in front of you. This way you can quickly and easily work through a known process and make a logical decision that not only makes sense to you, but is one you are confident you won't regret but will be very happy about.

Even if the outcome is not what you thought it would be, you'll know you made an educated decision. Let's face it, we're all going to be wrong some time and you can be okay with being wrong sometimes knowing that most of the time you worked to make decisions in your best interest. Rely on your system. You want to give yourself time to process important decisions. You've read about the 24-to-48 hour holding period. Let's make sure that does not happen during a period of 24-to-48 hours where you're so busy you don't even have time to think about the purchase. You need 24-to-48 hours where you do have quality time to reflect on the questions you need to ask. Go through your process, or whatever system you decide to follow, to help you get to a decision and get to a point where you feel confident that you've given everything ample time to sink in and consider. Maybe you can even consult people who know about the particular business opportunity product under consideration. Everything is available on Google; you might even search there to see what is good or not about a product.

With business opportunities, maybe you don't have that much time or maybe adequate information is not available on Google because an opportunity may be so new, but you can certainly give yourself the space to think about what the pros and cons might be and to look up similar types of business ventures and review what the pros and cons and results may have been. And of course, you can always consult your trusted adviser. Reach out to your financial strategist; tell them what you're facing. Is it a product or a service that you want to buy? Is it a business opportunity that you want to get involved in? Tell them about it. Allow them to walk you through the right questions. One strategy I use with clients, who aren't sure when to seek my help, is to establish a dollar amount for purchases or investments, where they agree to consult me first before making decisions above that amount.

Now, don't expect others to make the decision *for* you. In fact if you do, you're giving up your power, which, as we've clearly outlined before, is not the best way to reach your greatest goals. Don't give up your power to anyone. Use their resources and use their wisdom to help guide you

When setting up your financial future, a key area you will first engage is the decision to hire, or not hire, an agent. The first thing you need to know in this process is the purpose of hiring an agent in the first place. What will be the benefits? Why would you want an agent? What will you gain?

Once you have looked at why an agent is considered in the mix for a pro-athlete, then you can assess the pros and cons of having one. It may help you to create a list for yourself—to get very specific about how these benefits relate to your specific life.

One thing you may begin to notice is that as you begin to go pro, there will be all kinds of people ready to help you. It can get confusing and frustrating to try to figure out exactly who is really here to help you and who is here to help themselves. This is why building relationships and trust from the beginning is so important. You want the contract, and you want to play, but you also have to be concerned about your financial future as you embark on a unique career path. Figuring out who is really helping you may come down to relying on other key relationships in your life, especially from those who have nothing to gain based on your decisions, but may still have the experience and knowledge you need for guidance.

Mentors from your life may be helpful in times like these. Seek out the help from mentors who have helped get you to where you are. Often, those with experience are more than willing to help young people who show willingness and openness to learn and soak up their knowledge. Seek out a mentor if you do not have one… A great fit is someone who has the experience and nothing to gain but the satisfaction of your win. In addition to seeking out those professional mentors, it is critical you seek financial support from the beginning. In order to do that effectively, you need to know:

- Who will help you run numbers to see if the contract you are about to sign will support you reaching specific goals?
- Who will show you the total value you are signing over to an agent when you give up a portion of your salary for their services?
- Who will help you know what your actual take home pay is likely to be so you can know if the offer really is a good deal?
- With taxes in every state and all the other fees you likely face, who will help you calculate those numbers?

Get help from the start and you will
work way less later to reach your goals.

Put Together Your Team of Professionals

While all of the strategies we share here are important pieces of the overall puzzle to help you be as financially strong as possible, now and over your lifetime, one of the key strategies to help you put it all together is this one:

Hire Professionals!

Your job right now is to focus on the game. But how can you do that and be at your best performance while you are trying to figure out myriad money matters? There is great value in allowing those who are experts in an area to do their job.

By reading this Playbook, you are arming yourself with the base knowledge you need in order to know if you are being guided in the right direction. The goal is to have you sufficiently informed so you can know whom to trust when you put your financial future into someone else's hands. Knowing the basics means you are not just turning it over and hoping you did the right thing. Knowledge allows you to be involved enough and ask the right questions to be sure your team is doing what is right for you. Only when armed with knowledge can you confidently put your trusted advisors in place and return your focus on the game. This is the time to reflect on a few key considerations on which you want to focus as you build your financial team.

- Who should be on your team?
- What positions will they play?
- How do you find the right team for you?
- What questions can you ask to help see if they are a fit?

Who Should Be On Your Team?

Each situation may vary, but for most athletes, there are a few key players that should be on your team.

Agent—You have probably chosen an agent to help guide you through the process of going pro. In many cases, they have some key relationships in place already and can guide you to a financial team.

I caution you to be aware in this selection process, however, and know that a system of checks and balances may work in your favor if you choose to select your own financial advisors, independent from your agent. This is a personal choice, and when armed with the knowledge of this Playbook, you are at least better prepared to judge whether the team your agent already has in place is a fit for you. If you elect to go with the recommendations of your agent, get a second opinion just to be sure they are leading you on the right track. Reach out to our office; we are happy to be that second opinion for you. As a reader of this book, ask for our complementary **Second Look Review Package.**

Certified Public Accountant (CPA)—Your accountant will be a critical part of your team. This is the person who will calculate all the taxes you owe on your income. As a pro-athlete, you will be taxed in every state where you play. This can get messy; do not try to do this yourself, and while you love mom, she is not the person for this (unless she is a practicing accountant in this area of expertise of course).

Your accountant can keep you out of a heap of trouble and save you thousands by helping you find all of the tax advantages available to you. Your CPA can only work for you as much as you give them information, though. If you start a home-based business, you have to turn in your receipts and let them know what transactions occurred so they can get you the best deductions. I suggest a separate account where your accountant can log in and check your transactions. Make your life easy and get a card just for tax deductible spending and help your CPA help you.

Do you remember the scenes in the movie, Jerry Maguire? Not the one about "show me the money," but when he goes to the depth of emotion and tells Rod Tidwell, "I am out here for you. You don't know what it's like to be *me* out here for *you*! It is an up-at-dawn, pride-swallowing siege that I will never fully tell you about, ok?" And, then... the more poignant moment as he beseeches Tidwell, saying, "Help me... help you. Help me, help you!"

This is the support you deserve and need to find!

◇◇◇◇◇◇◇◇◇◇◇◇◇

Certified Financial Planner™ (CFP®)—Your CFP® will be the go-to-person to help you choose the financial strategies best suited for you. This can be any financial strategist, but you want to look for those who have the credentials to help you. If not a CFP®, then find someone with a similar credential like a Personal Financial Specialist (PFS) or a Chartered Financial Analyst (CFA). These are among the most rigorous credentials to achieve. You may choose a CFP® or PFS to work with individually; it is not likely you will work with a CFA as they typically manage large funds rather than individual accounts. Your financial advisor can also guide you to the right team to help you focus on your investment needs such a Registered Investment Advisor (RIA).

Estate Planner—Your estate planner likely comes in the form of an attorney or a CFP®/CPA with attorney partnerships. Estate planning attorneys can guide you in the use of Trusts and other products that may further meet your ultimate desires for building your estate. An estate, by definition, is all the assets you have, and estate planning is choosing to whom you will leave those when you leave the earth.

Once you have assembled your base team candidates, you start asking questions to help you determine if they are the right fit for you. Some important questions to ask are the following.

- What are your fees and how do you get paid if I work with you?
- What are your investment philosophies?
- How can you help me?
- How long have you been in business? What are your credentials?
- What are some examples of people you have helped?
- How much interaction do you have with your clients?
- How can I access you?
- Who all is on your team and will be helping with my planning process?
- How often do you revisit and revise your clients' accounts?

- Who is your target client?
- What makes you unique to work with me above other planners?

These questions are designed to help you assess whether a particular planner has the right attitude, credentials, and longevity to work with you. For instance, when asking for credentials, you are looking for advisors who are fiduciary advisors. This means they have to put your interests above their own when advising you. Most highly credentialed individuals, such as CFP's and CPA's took an oath to do this in order to gain their certification.

You also look for creative ideas about how they can help you, and to see that their innate creativity is a match for what you want. For instance, if you sense your advisor is a huge risk taker and you are not, it may not be a good long-term fit. Likewise, if you want to take tons of risks and chances to grow your assets more quickly, an advisor who is all about low risk strategies may not be a fit. Look for someone who talks about focusing the plan on the client, not only his or her personal ideas of what is best. For example, I personally like taking advantage of both worlds: low risk with moderate but steady returns. However, if I have a client who wants to work with what we call earlier in this Playbook play money to take larger risks and get some bigger gains, I generally connect them with members of my team who specialize in that area, at least for this part of their planning strategy.

You may find that the financial strategist you interview has several packages to offer, depending on your needs. For instance, if you want an annual review only, there may be a fee package for that, plus the potential to earn commissions on some products that may be a good fit for you. If you want more access, you can normally purchase a different package, which allows for that.

In my client base, we have clientele who receive reviews as infrequently as annually; their intent is to maintain lower fees. At the same time, I manage a small number of openings for my highest interactive clients... the ones who want to have me on speed dial for every financial decision they make. Since this is so highly interactive, there is a limit on how many of these clients I can have at a time, and they are happy to pay my highest fees for this added handholding. These clients do not consider the fees excessive; they realize how much it saves them by just checking with me first to evaluate the overall impact of each decision on their financial future. This makes sense to these often spend-thrifty clients. However, it just wouldn't make sense for some of my clients who have a solid understanding of how their decisions affect them and have the behavior patterns to act accordingly. Look for a strategist who will be flexible, and can personally meet your specific desires and needs.

Once you have selected your team, it is now time to create an action plan together. This is where you want to communicate all of your desires, needs, and aspirations to your team. Get them involved in your desired spending patterns, let them know the lifestyle you want to live now and in the future, and involve them in your big dream goals. You may be surprised how you can reach your dream goals by simply telling your team you have them! They can likely help you work out a plan to reach it, and surprise you with how it may be more easily achieved than you think... with proper planning. Communicate thoroughly and often with your team and you will be very pleased with your results.

Chapter 19

STRATEGY #9: BE SURE YOU ENJOY THE JOURNEY

IN THIS SECTION, we want to cover the importance of enjoying the journey along the way. Can you imagine going through your entire sporting career and never enjoy playing the game? It's hard to imagine, isn't it? That's why you chose this career in the first place, isn't it? You really enjoyed the game and you were good, so why not maximize those skills; build them and do what you need to do to get into a sport and into a game where you can literally love every day of your life.

Well, the same thing is supposed to happen with your money path. The idea is to remember it's supposed to be enjoyable, this whole thing... the journey you're on, the game you're playing, the money you're making... it is supposed to be fun, but it can be overwhelming. I know this, and this awareness is why I do what I do and why I write to share my wisdom and expertise.

I've seen so many people come through my office doors; they feel like money has single-handedly created craziness in their lives and they begin to wonder if having money is really all it was cracked up to be, or all they ever thought it would be. But the truth is—*it is supposed to be fun*. While it can appear complicated, with the right guidance, it really doesn't have to be. So agree to allow it to be fun. It's not your job to know every single investment and where your money should be at any given time.

Should you understand what's going on with your money? Absolutely. But do you have to understand every nuance, every detail? Or do you really just need to build relationships where you trust professionals who can explain enough to you so you can understand the basics of what's going on. You're supposed to be having fun with life. You have reached a milestone that so many dream of… and so few reach. Enjoy it. Bask in the energy of knowing that you have arrived, and let yourself think, *Good job. Way to go.* Go ahead, take your atta boys and enjoy it. Let it be fun!

When you headed here, how did you get here? Let's go back to think about that because your financial journey is, in fact, very similar to the journey that you were on to get you into pro games.

- The first thing you learned to do was train hard.
- You practiced. You probably practiced more than other kids around you.
- You gave it more energy, more effort, more focus.
- You were watching film when everyone else was watching movies.
- You were improving and practicing the same move over and over and over whenever everyone else was drinking beer and eating wings.
- You put in the work.

Good job and reward yourself for it. But the truth is, what did you get to do as a result? You trained hard so you got to play even harder. You got to be involved in a game when everyone else said, Well, yeah, I'd love to go pro, but you did it.

You did it... when no one else around you could or did!

◇◇◇◇◇◇◇◇◇◇◇◇◇◇

So when it comes to your money, you take those same pro-athlete-skills and you've got to train equally hard. Now... you will get to play even harder. The coolest part about that, because you trained hard and smart, you get to play hard throughout your entire life—not just on the field— but in your entire life. There are rewards, financial and otherwise, and you get to enjoy them because of playing smart. When you play hard in the money game and make smart decisions along the way, you also get to play for life.

Does that mean you're going to be on the field or playing your pro game for the rest of your life? Who knows? Maybe there's something else you'll be passionate about and get involved in, but you still get to play in the game (of life) even after you retire. Maybe you'll move on and choose not to participate in any kind sports, but to watch and enjoy others play. However, many pro-athletes, I imagine, will jump on the chance to get involved in the next game when the opportunity arises—at least on a casual level—even after retirement. But the truth is, it does not matter if you play again or not?

YOU get to enjoy the choice!

◇◇◇◇◇◇◇◇◇◇◇◇◇◇

A choice is one of the biggest things that you will have earned by elevating yourself to a pro-athlete position. Remember, you're here to enjoy the journey. So make sure you do!

Let me get real visible and vulnerable here and share with you some of the things that I've experienced and seen happen along my own journey. The truth is if you lose track of the joy in the game, you're probably going to want to start filling it with the stuff and things of life. So imagine you made it to this point and you get involved in the game, and then you find out all of the pitfalls that go with being a pro ball player. Nobody told you all the pros and cons when you were training hard and trying to get into the game when you were looking through a track, or trying to make the cut and hit the *Big Time*.

No one told you about all of the details, all of the contracts, all the things you were now going to have to face, all of the rules you were going to have to follow in order to stay involved in the game, or all the fines you might have to pay if you mess up. Am I right? No one ever talked about those aspects of the life you chose. The focus was on encouraging you to... Just hit it! Just hit the big game; just hit the *Big Time*. Well, the same thing applies to your financial game. When you really go for it, you similarly focus on the bigger vision, with a greater awareness:

- What's it going to be like?
- Where are you going to live?
- What kind of stuff (life materials) are you going to have?

When in the midst of a pro ball game, it is easy to get so focused on the plays, you might forget to enjoy the process. The results of the game itself are your reward, right? Forget the details and the loopholes and the fines and the charges. The truth is you're here to play a game; a game you play well, and are paid well to do it.

When you go after your financial dreams and look at what you want, you might find yourself caught up in the I'll be happy when theme. Let me assure you, that's one of the biggest mistakes you can make. I urge you, if you ever catch yourself using that phrase, and it is likely you will, keep alerted to trigger words to look for:

- Well, I'll be happy as soon as…
- I'll be happy when this happens…
- Once I get… I can be happy.
- When… happens, I'll feel good.

If you get in the habit of setting your emotions on some future occurrence that you wait to have happen, the chances of you ever truly attaining happiness are very low. Let's face it. You probably thought, *I'll be happy when I go pro*. And as soon as you attained that goal, all of these other pieces come to the surface and next thing you know, you are off on the, Well, I'll be happy when I'm on the starting team theme. Next you will hear yourself say, Well, I'll be happy when I reach MVP. Then, when you accomplish that, now what? The truth is… all of these goals are great. You want to have goals to work toward.

Don't let the goals you work toward steal from you the beauty and the joy of what you have right now because this, my friend, all of this is the game; all of this is your journey.

This message is probably the most important piece of wisdom I am passionate to share! I heard a mentor of mine speak recently, one of the best presentations I've ever heard him give. He said,

You know, the moment, that moment when you've reached the goal that you set. You've reached the rank you worked for. You've reached the position

you've strived for. You've reached the number of touchdowns you hoped to score. You've reached that moment. That is but a moment and you get a fraction of a second where that moment is being reached. Everything else is the journey to that moment.

I encourage you to remember the emphasis on the last line…

Everything else is the journey to that moment.

◇◇◇◇◇◇◇◇◇◇◇◇◇

When you think about your goals, if you are only focused on the moment of accomplishing any given goal, you can very well miss all of the beauty of the journey of getting there. How much fun would it be for you if you could just grab the ball and run across the finish line and win? Or is it more of the joy because to get there you had obstacles to face, you had people to go through, and you had other people trying to stop you from reaching that goal. You made the goal in spite of all that, and in many cases you made it, because of your determination to get through all of it. If you think about that, how boring would any game be if you didn't have opposing teams and obstacles, or something that challenged you to finally cross a finish line?

The same thing can apply to your financial game… there are obstacles; there are others taking a stand against you. There are people who want take your money right out of your pocket and put it in their own. There are markets that go up and down, and material items you think you need and want. There are times you will blow money and feel like you wasted something precious, and there are moments you will not make the best choices; focus only on the moments when you will.

At the end of your contract (with life), put all of those moments together, each of them doing the best you can, going, continuing, messing up and getting back out there—again and picking up what you can and going through the next round, doing the next play, running the next race… all of pieces of life together represent the entire journey… but that moment will arrive when you can look at your numbers and say, I am fully financially free and for the rest of my life, I won't have to work if I don't want to. When that moment comes, it is but a singular moment, but it's a beautiful, wonderful one that will ultimately lead to many others. The truth is, though, you don't have to wait for that moment to enjoy this part of your *life game* because it's the decisions made day after day that make a difference.

It's the moment you walk away from some purchase because what you see for your life is so much grander than this one thing that you thought to buy right now. It's the moment you walk away with your head held high, your confidence soaring and feeling good about the congruency of your visions, disciplines and choices. Those are the moments that make all this worth it.

If you lose the joy in the journey, you will for sure fade away and fail to reach your big moment. I want to repeat that because for some of you, it may not immediately sink in as much as it needs to.

> *If you fail to enjoy the journey, you will*
> *most likely fail to reach your big moment.*

<>◇◇◇◇◇◇◇◇◇◇◇◇◇◇<>

That *one moment of accomplishment* is made up of all of the moments along your journey so you may experience that *one moment*. Understand this: You may finally reach the financial freedom you seek; you may finally reach the goal to become MVP, but if you didn't learn to enjoy the journey to getting there, you're going to miss the joy of life's game. You'll be in the game all right; it will happen, but you really won't be present when *the moment* occurs. These are the moments you look for your entire life and you really don't want to miss that fraction of a second when you actually reach where you're headed.

Don't lose track of your choice. Stay on target. Stay in direct connection to the why and the journey and the moment. You've heard the phrase, Stop and smell the roses. This is your roses. Your journey— the steps and the daily decisions you make to take you where you want to be.

That's the journey; you've got to enjoy it, for that,
my friend, is where the true wealth comes into play.

◇◇◇◇◇◇◇◇◇◇◇◇◇

There's one more thing I want to share with you about enjoying the journey, which I found was critical in my own life. I wrote about whether you lose track of the joy, and how you may want to feed that emptiness with material things and countless other stuff. What happens when you let go of the joy and no longer enjoy the journey is an overwhelming need for stuff. Just what do I consider stuff? The stuff includes items, which may have little to no value in your life, or don't contribute significantly to your overall pleasure. What they accomplish is to give you a little bit of pleasure right now, which leads you to just *go for it* because you're so empty and you've got to feed that emptiness.

I write to you based on personal experience. I was very young when I got married. In fact, I was 17 when I had my first son, but was 19 when I married the man who had been my boyfriend since 13. I married him because it was the right thing to do and was all I knew at the time. I was fixed on some terrible idea I had heard somewhere in my very young life, "You made this bed; it's your job to lie in it." What a terrible phrase! I finally thought, *How about you unmake that bed and do it again?* But there I was, and at 19, what could I expect? I didn't know any better, right? I'm just grateful I know now.

Marriage at best is difficult, and as often happens in marriages, people discover the desire and the right to be happy within them. I discovered

I, too, wanted to be happy. Now add another layer to my story… in that I live my life as a typically optimistic person. This translated to periods of time I convinced myself I *was* happy so I could then *feel* happy. So life carried on:

- it was basically good and even though my husband wasn't the right match for me…
- even though it wasn't the right situation for me…
- even the circumstances that led us to marriage, were not the ones that I would have chosen had I felt I had any control at that time, but…
- here I found myself making the best of life.

Unfortunately, the truth is: you can only fool yourself for so long before the truth surfaces, and the truth was: I was not happy and my thoughts rambled.

- We are not a good marriage match; we weren't from the beginning, and we still don't fit.
- I have expansive thought processes and my personality is to go and do beyond anything that I am right now.
- I need to grow spiritually, emotionally, socially and intellectually and a plethora of other areas where I need growth to survive.
- He is comfortable with what we have—and not that one is right and the other wrong—but he is too comfortable with consistency and being set and just sticking to the known… the comfortable… the secure.

When a couple's views are that different, things start to happen, which create problems within the relationship, but because I didn't want our reality to be true, I started to mask it.

I was unhappy and as I tried to mask the idea of being unhappy, the problem manifested itself in my wanting stuff. Now, up until this point, I had always been a saver. In fact, I was the saver who married a spender, so we rarely had extra money left over except what I would hide from him to save for retirement and other purposes because I was financially astute; I knew money. But when I became honest with being unhappy, all of sudden, I became a spender, too. What started to happen is:

- I wanted a new car…
- I wanted a new house…
- I wanted, wanted, wanted.

Actually, we had the means for me to have a lot of these things but the problem became bigger than myself as the newer car and the bigger house soon failed to be enough. Then my happiness showed up in wanting more clothes, and then I wanted more stuff for the two boys I now had. A master at controlling me, my unhappiness let to an excruciating need for new handbags—often—then I needed to travel and I needed to go do things and before I knew it…there was never even the remotest feeling of being satisfied.

My thinking was always, *I'll be happy when I get these things.* For several years, I lived under the theme of I'll be happy when… but each need quickly turned into the next thing… and the next thing… and the next thing. I noticed every time I accomplished the *next thing* that was supposed to make me happy, something else was revealed that I needed first, only after which I was going to be happy.

It wasn't until I finally acknowledged I was just not happy with the basic circumstances of my life and it wasn't at all the lack of stuff in my life that impeded my happiness that I actually walked away from all of it. I gave it all up… all the *stuff* I thought all those years I needed to be happy… I walked away from it all and found out happiness could only be found inside of me.

I share this story with you so that you can understand that if you feel that emptiness… that longing… that need for more… it is a clear sign it is time to dig deeply and explore what's really going on. Many times living the wrong happiness theme could be one of the biggest areas of sabotage to your financial goals. Find where you're not happy in something; focus on what makes you happy.

Stop! Consider what there is about this part of your life journey you can enjoy and love and maybe discover the areas of your life you need to change. Maybe it's just a new perspective. Living life itself is good, but you thought you had to reach all of these goals before you could be happy. Allow yourself to embrace joy now because not doing so can be of the biggest saboteurs of your financial life.

Try this one for me. I don't want to sound like a broken record about this topic, but it is so prevalent, destructive, and hidden deep within us, I am compelled to push at the limits of awareness and understanding. When you question or ask yourself what it takes to be happy… anytime you say, I'll be happy when. As soon as this happens, I can relax. Or any similar phrase, promise as soon as you catch yourself, you will pause and go back to your question and change it to, 'What would it take for me to be happy now?' The moment you are willing and able to answer that specific question, you will enjoy your life journey so much more, you will find your experiences far richer, and most importantly, your financial life will benefit.

Chapter 20

CONCLUSION

WHEN IT COMES to your money, there is no substitute for gaining the knowledge and making sure you have participated in taking care of your future. By now, you are more likely than others in your position to avoid the top five mistakes, simply by having become informed. If you continue to avoid the mistakes outlined here and continue to build upon the nine strategies, you are headed toward a powerful, and financially successful future.

The principles you have learned here remind you to take action in *seven key areas:*

1. Think ahead regarding your financial future.
2. Plan for a life you want during and after your game years.
3. Make powerful investment choices with clear goals in mind.
4. Remain in control of your financial picture.

5. Give and help others along the way.
6. Seek professional help so you can focus on your game.
7. Enjoy your life journey. You only get one shot at it.

We look forward to hearing your success stories as you follow these principles. As you embark on this journey, keep in mind these powerful tips when you need the guidance to keep going, and refer back to this Playbook as often as needed. Take it with you to your appointments, and contact our office any time you need more support.

Rock on, Superstar. Welcome to the Big Time!

ABOUT THE AUTHOR

Dr. Crystal D. Gifford, CFP® has been teaching and serving in the financial industry since 1999. As a young mother, she recognized very quickly that it was important to understand financial matters, which prompted her to focus her attention on Finance and Accounting in college. Pursuing this career, Crystal spent years building experience advising and educating others, eventually building her own practice. Her own life experiences led her on a mission to save others from suffering devastating financial losses.

Crystal's focus on professional athletes was sparked by classroom interactions in 2007 when she was a college professor at a HBCU (Historically Black Colleges and Universities) school where she guided some of her student athletes as they stepped into professional careers. Since then, she has grown this support for athletes to a powerful platform providing financial education and development, leading many to financial freedom.

During her term at this University, Crystal decided to complete her doctorate in Accounting and become a Certified Financial Planner™. With the credentials to support her experience, she then expanded her classroom teaching to support high-income earners in crafting a clear and manageable plan for a lifetime of wealth.

Dr. Gifford currently educates professional and college athletes on money matters with her book tour for *The Money Shot: The Professional Athlete's Playbook to Make the Big Time Last a* Lifetime. As a keynote speaker and workshop educator she helps foster awareness for athletes guiding them through the difficult and unclear financial maze. Dr. Gifford excels at educating her clients on how to make powerful money decisions in the real world.

BOOK DR. GIFFORD

To book Dr. Gifford as a speaker for your group, or discover for more resources, tools, and tips—visit www.financialdevelopment.org and enter your contact information so you may stay up to date with her latest releases.

CRYSTAL OFFERS SOLUTIONS

A path to financial freedom.
A guilt-free, sustainable life of luxury.
The onramp to bring dreams into reality and sustain that dream.
Overcome the overwhelm that often comes with money matters.
Build your income while saving you time.
Live the life you thought you could only dream of living—without breaking the bank.
Making the Big Time Last a Lifetime—for high-income earners who want to make sure success lasts.

A complimentary luxurious living consultation awaits you at
<u>www.financialdevelopment.org</u>

THANK YOU!

... for reading *The Money Shot*. We trust you have not only enjoyed these rich possibilities for... a real look into the world of a professional athlete and how this new-found fame and fortune can change their lives. Walking through the financial maze can be challenging for athletes who really need to focus on game performance. The tips and tools in *The Money Shot* allows athletes and their families to clearly identify how to find success in the money game so they can focus on career success as an athlete. Exploring the "do's" and "don'ts" of saving, spending, using, and growing money, *The Money Shot* is designed to provide the roadmap to successful financial performance by laying out the steps play-by-play. Athletes and their families gain knowledge to make the right moves for their financial present and future, and confidence to know they are performing at peak levels in the money game

Thank you in advance for taking the time to post a review for the book on Amazon; many readers will not take that step to purchase and read... until they know someone else has led the way.

If you enjoyed reading *The Money Shot* I would appreciated it if you would help others enjoy the book, too.

LEND IT. This book is lending enabled, so please feel free to share with a friend.

RECOMMEND IT. Please help other readers find the book by recommending it to readers' groups, discussion boards, Goodreads, etc.

REVIEW IT. Please tell others why you liked this book by reviewing it on the site where you purchased it, on your favorite book site, or your own blog.

EMAIL ME. I'd love to hear from you.

crystal@crystalgifford.com

www.financialdevelopment.org

If you would like to be the first to read my upcoming books, subscribe to my VIP READERS.

OTHER BOOKS BY DR. GIFFORD

{An} Unsinkable Soul: The Phoenix Lives Again

Quite frankly… life happens! In *{An} Unsinkable Soul* readers will find stories by purpose-directed authors who have learned to bounce back from life's challenges, creating Unsinkable concepts they have come to live… as dynamic and transformational experts who want to lead others to a better place in what we call LIFE! {An} Unsinkable Soul was written to provide and encourage readers to look differently at life challenges, and in bouncing back from them… to continue moving forward. At the end of the day, readers will find hope and love in the midst of chaos and uncertainty.

AMAZON: http://www.amazon.com/dp/0615970176

KINDLE: http://www.amazon.com/dp/B00IFUXJJQ

Live Sassy Formula: Make Big Money and a Big Difference Doing What You Love!

You know in your heart… there's a bigger plan for your life

AMAZON: http://www.amazon.com/dp/B00DIL0KDK

The Money Makeover: How to Easily Get Out of Debt, Create Wealth, and Leverage Passive Income

Business and Economics or Personal Finance... Money Management is key to living real financial freedom—and it comes in the form of this personal and practical guide, *The Money Makeover.*

In *The Money Makeover*, Dr. Crystal Dawn Gifford takes you through nine simple steps, each designed to help you reduce debt, create successful long-term financial strategies, and give you the real secrets to success, happiness, and wealth.

This book is a definite GAME CHANGER...

It is also the publication that led Dr. Gifford to establish The International Center for Athletic Financial Development™ to guide college and professional athletes to powerful financial strategies that allow them to fully enjoy their earnings both now and in the future.

AMAZON: http://www.amazon.com/dp/0996297200

KINDLE: http://www.amazon.com/dp/B0131UEB8C

RESOURCES

The information is written exclusively from the expertise and experience of Dr. Crystal Dawn Gifford, CFP®

You were provided different connection points throughout the book. They are repeated here for your convenience:

crystal@crystalgifford.com
www.crystalgifford.com
www.empoweredgift.com
www.financialdevelopment.org
www.yescrystal.com

Before you go, you owe it to yourself to gain access to my five secrets to turning you cash flow into abundant wealth today at
www.empoweredgift.com

Printed in the USA
CPSIA information can be obtained
at www.ICGtesting.com
JSHW022331140824
68134JS00019B/1422

9 781630 478377